SUPER
PERFORMANCE

New Profound Knowledge for Corporate Leaders

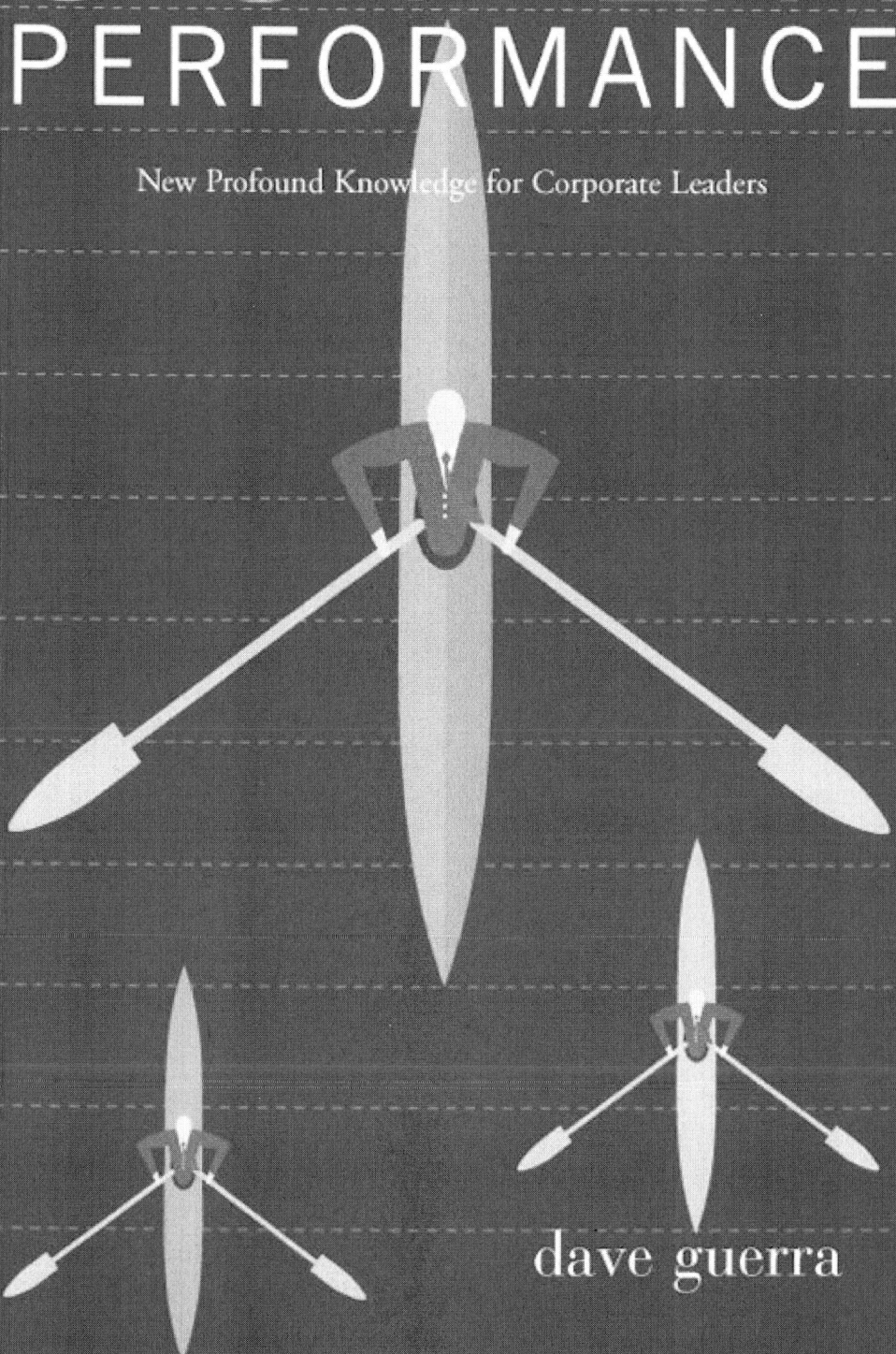

dave guerra

MW01514528

SUPER
PERFORMANCE

New Profound Knowledge for Corporate Leaders

---

1 Simple Formula

8 Simple Rules

1 Billion Great Results

Dave Guerra

Copyright © 2005 Dave Guerra
All rights reserved
Printed in the United States of America

This book may not be reproduced, stored in a retrieval system, or transmitted in whole or in part, in any form or by any means, electronic, mechanical, photocopying, recording, or otherwise, without the prior written permission of Dave Guerra.

OLD LIVE
OAK BOOKS

Cover Design by Axiom Design Group, Houston, Texas.

Library of Congress Catalog Card Number 2005906413
Guerra, Dave
    Superperformance: New Profound Knowledge for Corporate Leaders

ISBN 1-58961-396-1

This book is
Dedicated to my mother
Virginia Sanchez Guerra
Whose Indomitable Spirit and Fiery Passion
Lives on in these Pages

Contents

Preface

Having worked in the Quality field for several decades, one thing has become obvious. Performance eludes most organizations. Even after Deming, even after Six Sigma, Self-Directed Work Teams, Reengineering, and Human Performance Technology, sustainable performance excellence remains out of reach.

Some companies seem to have the answer. We've tried to copy them, through the use of best practices, to replicate their techniques, but to no avail. Most of us remain disappointed and dissatisfied.

Could it be there is something else, something *simpler* driving their success?

> Simplicity is removing the unnecessary so the necessary can speak.
>
> WILLIAM JAMES

In 1990 Michael Rothschild published an important book entitled *Bionomics: Economy as Ecosystem.*[1] The book postulated that the economy is in reality an ecosystem inhabited by organizations that are in reality biological organisms. A few years later Margaret Wheatley published another groundbreaking book entitled *Leadership and the New Science*, proposing instead that organizations are

Go from your
CURRENT STATE   to   **SUPERPERFORMANCE**

| STATE 1 | → | STATE 2 |

Achieve Dramatic Results
Cultivate Excellence
Restore People
Transform Performance
Optimize Your Organization
Simplify Your Worklife

complex adaptive systems (CAS).[2] I assert that both of these statements are true. Organizations are both biological *and* complex adaptive organisms.

This may seem a trivial statement to make, but in reality it is revolutionary. It leads to a new management science, a new set of guiding principles, and a new theory of optimization, informed by a deep appreciation for the biology and physics at work in all organizations.

Nothing is too wonderful to be true.

MICHAEL FARADAY

Seeing organizations in this new way (as biological, complex adaptive organisms) changes how we define management and leadership. It makes Superperformance attainable and easy to understand—revealing a direct path to transformation.

Taking this path leads to a new understanding for how organizations work, an exciting new view of corporate culture, and a deeper inquiry into the *nature* of organizations.

Based on this knowledge, my aim is to equip you with a new paradigm and toolset for catalyzing Superperformance in your own organization, regardless of its size. The following pages include an operational definition of Superperformance, the Superperformance Formula, and the qualitative and quantitative data to prove that it works. This includes the evidence of ten organizational Superperformers and the outline of eight simple rules for transformation to this remarkable, new steady state.

Dave Guerra
August 1, 2005
Houston

Acknowledgements

In the original Superman series, the Bizarro Superman World was a place where everything worked backwards. In this world nothing made sense—coming was going, wrong was right, sense was nonsense. Everything was topsy-turvy on this planet.

Increasingly, the business world has seemed so to me. Wall Street's insatiable appetite for short-term profits, environments of win-lose competition, strictly numbers-based management, fear-based environments, rampant, applauded layoffs, forced ranking, 'toxic' employees, and on and on. The resulting attitude of "every man for himself" has seemed so hopelessly destructive. But like in Bizarro Superman World, when everyone around you is behaving as if this is normal, as if this is what makes sense, it is easy to feel that *it is you* who are crazy, *it is you* who has it wrong.

Occasionally I would stumble across the rare leader whose manner and actions cut against the grain of corporate convention. These people fit a surprising pattern: they were always humble, bona fide servant leaders who cared about people, they were always ferocious quality champions, and they always seemed to be exemplars of wisdom, grace…and simplicity.

It began to dawn on me that the performance of their organizations fit a pattern too. An amazing, consistent pattern.

It was these anomalies that pointed the way for me out of Bizarro Superman World and into the world of Superperformance.

For this, I am eternally grateful to my own father Robert Guerra, cofounder and Chairman of San Antonio's City Employees Federal Credit Union, Ed Roberson, Chairman and founder of Houston Northwest Medical Center, John Adams, CEO of Denton Cooley's Cardiovascular Care Providers, the late Ted Bauer, cofounder and former CEO and Chairman of AIM Investments, Jeff Holland, CEO of West Houston Medical Center, and George Martinez, cofounder and former CEO and Chairman of Sterling Bank.

I salute you, along with the other top leaders of the Superperforming companies profiled in these pages. We must continue to learn from you and others like you what Superperformance is, and not just how to get it but how to keep it—this elusive steady state.

Certainly this book would not have been possible without the context of an underlying new science. As such, it is an honor to pay my respects to those intellectual giants that have most informed my own learning. I am mostly indebted to the work of W. Edwards Deming, but also, on the biological side, to Ludwig Bertalanffy, Michael Rothschild, and Royal Dutch Shell's Arie De Geus, while on the complexity side I am thankful for the work of Illya Prigogene, John Holland, Stuart Kauffman, Fritjof Capra, and of course, Meg Wheatley, for her introduction of these concepts to organizations. Closer to home I am grateful for the mastery and guidance of quality improvement experts Lloyd Provost, David Wayne, and Pat Nahas, organizational complexity master Chris Welsh, and emotional intelligence guru Judy Campbell.

Making a book is an amazing process. The author's role is greatly diminished in the latter stages, when manuscripts are reviewed, polished and laid out, book covers designed and developed, and every last granular detail checked and rechecked. Throughout all of this experience this book has been blessed by the excellent work of so many people. For reviewing the manuscript I am especially grateful to Bambi McCullough, Sharon and Stewart Jacobson, Robert Belew, Laura Eaton, Gregg Stocker, Kevin Gallagher, Jim Dale, Luzanne Coburn, Joe Browne, Sivasailam Thiagarajan ("Thiagi"), Matthew Marion, David Germain, and Barry Curtis. I am deeply grateful to my editor, Linda Nuttall for elevating the book to an unexpected level, and to Kent Nuttall, for his painstaking attention to detail as the book became an exercise in granularity. I also am indebted to David Lerch for the predictably simple but elegant book cover and page design.

In addition, I would be remiss for failing to mention my gratitude to other special encouragers and promoters of this work including my agent Christine Brown of Global Speakers Agency, Rich Cozart, my friend and pastor, Rodger Marty, Chris Gianakos, Mary Gerstner, Larry Doiron, Susan Zeigle, Amie Close, LaShawnda Johnson, Luke Davis, Matt Crowder, and Hewlett Packard's Teresa Ratliff, Corpus Optima's original corporate customer many years ago.

On a more personal front I would like to acknowledge my wonderful wife Jodi and my beautiful children Carmen, Luke, Paulina, and Danielle, whom I have most to thank for my sweet, sweet life. Thank you for your patience and understanding throughout my countless hours of work away from you.

In conclusion I should also reveal that the word "superperformance" came to me in prayer. And so I am most grateful to God that when you ask, you receive and that all things are possible to him that believes.

The Formula, The Evidence, and the Science of Superperformance

8 Simple Rules

RULE 1:   Process x Culture = Superperformance

Chapter 1

How Superperformance Happens

What is Organizational Superperformance?

Organizational Superperformance is a measure of value. It is defined as industry-outperforming return on investment (ROI) sustained over time (at least a dozen years). Time turns out to be a critical distinction, as outperformance so rarely lasts.

Against this yardstick only a precious few stand out from the trivial many to qualify as Superperformers. Every Superperforming company has evolved adaptations that provide valuable, distinct advantages in its

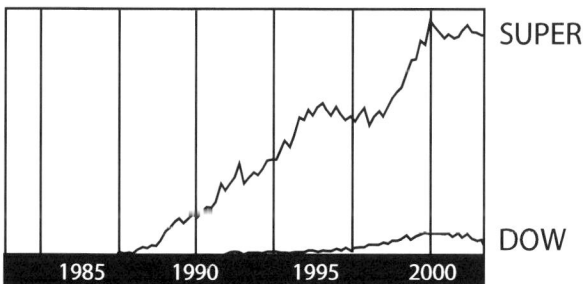

Superperformance vs. DOW
1985 - 2005

3

field. Studying Superperformers as a group reveals an amazingly consistent pattern, and the discovery of a new steady state. By understanding and adopting a few simple rules, any organization can make the shift to Superperformance.

Superperformance is Not Flash Performance

Superperformance is not flash performance. Flash performance comes from a string of strategies *du jour*, where results seem promising at first, but mostly fall back to previous levels—with a resulting loss of energy. These generic strategies focus on short-term results; they come from mechanistic cause-and-effect mindsets.

Typically, flash performance produces analgesic relief—followed by even greater problems.

Flash Performance:
- Fizzles out.
- Fails to achieve transformation.
- Often masks underlying root causes leading to greater problems later.
- Disengages people.

Flash performance is driven by expedience. Its strategies are designed to fix a current problem, relieve some pressure, or merely create a false impression of immediately improved performance to satisfy some constituency (e.g., Wall Street).

Flash performance affirms mediocrity, compromises quality, and, in the extreme, leads to ethical lapses and flawed decision making. There are numerous recent examples of spectacular business failures whose grand strategies turned out to be no more than flash performance. The most egregious are the legion of high-flying Internet companies now vanished from the landscape, as well as several formerly vaunted blue chips (Enron, WorldCom, etc.).

But the truth is that flash performance is the standard of practice in most organizations today. The almighty "next quarter number" trumps any other priority.

True Superperformers recognize that a few quarters (and sometimes even a few years) of great numbers might still turn out to be flash performance. Superperformance requires systemic transformation, not bandages.

Hidden Simplicity

To understand Superperformance is to see organizations in a remarkable new way. Superperformance emerges *for free* in organizations that can learn and apply a few simple rules. These rules leverage inherent properties found in all organizations. But the fundamental mechanism that begets Superperformance is impossible to recognize and put to good use without a shift in worldview.

> Not everything that counts can be counted. And not everything that can be counted, counts.
>
> ALBERT EINSTEIN

Our worldview influences everything we experience, including life in organizations. A change in worldview can lead in some unexpectedly new and different directions, sometimes provoking a new interpretation and response to the reality we inhabit. The simple wisdom of Superperformance has been mostly hidden, thanks to our lingering mechanistic paradigm. When we see that an organization is actually an organism—a real living system—we can finally see the true pattern of Superperformance.

The Superperformance Formula

The Superperformance spark is struck between an organization's work and its passion. It springs from the intersection of these two forces, in the sweet spot between the physical and emotional organization.

RULE 1:   Process x Culture = Superperformance

The Superperformance Formula (PxC=SP) is easy to understand and apply:

Process x Culture = Superperformance

Superperformance is the product of process and culture. In this formula "process" is defined as the work and "culture" is defined as the spirit of an organization. The *work* of an organization comprises its physical dimension—encompassing business strategies, systems, and methods. The *spirit* of an organization reflects the creativity, engagement, and inspiration of people in the company—its emotional dimension. The

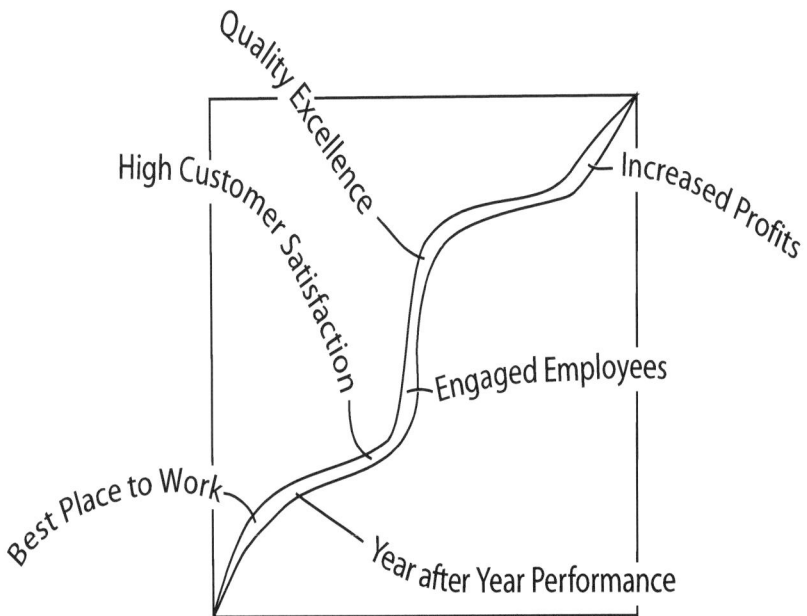

The Emergence of Superperformance

strength and interaction of these two forces alone catalyze organizational Superperformance.

Process	x	Culture	=	Superperformance
Systems		Commitment		Customer Delight
Structures		Values		Quality Excellence
Methods		Engagement		Long Term Value
Strategy		Inspiration		Outperforming ROI
				Employee Joy in Work

In the language of Superperformance, process and culture are *polar-complements*; they oppose each other but also need each other for completion. Superperformers treat process and culture as dual hemispheres—two halves of one outperforming whole.

This point is crucial and bears repeating. The critical distinction is that Superperformers treat process and culture as dual hemispheres—two halves of one outperforming whole.

Most organizational sub-performance comes from focusing only on the process side of the equation—the physical dimension. This orientation is a holdover from Machine View, a concept we'll explore in depth in Chapter 3. Operating the organization as a machine encourages flash performance—driving expedient behavior, extinguishing joy in work, and making things worse. This is the equivalent of operating with only half a brain (the left). The effect is as damaging to an organization as it would be to you or to me. To achieve Superperformance, it is necessary to fully employ both hemispheres.

How the Formula Works

Applying the Superperformance formula (P x C – 3P) to an organization is a straightforward process. Imagine a perfect score of 100 possible for an organization with a fully optimized process (10) and culture (10). To approach transformation, a proposed minimum score of 5 is required in each dimension, with a product of 50 representing the tipping point of Superperformance. On a scale from 1-10, most organizations today are decidedly out of balance, with a significantly higher score in process than in culture.

In a typical organization we might see the following results:

Process x Culture = Mediocre Results
7   x   3   =   21

The common approach for such an organization striving to improve performance would be to focus even more resolutely on process. But the potential for a much larger gain would come from enhancing the culture. Why? It would be much more difficult to ratchet up the process dimension without the actual engagement of the people who do the work itself. Unfortunately, this is exactly what most organizations try to do.

Instead, a purposeful campaign to create an authentic sense of process ownership—through enrolling, developing, and empowering people— would render a much larger gain. The result of such a campaign may look something like this:

Process x Culture = Approaching Breakpoint
7   x   7   =   49

Conversely, the rare organization reflecting higher performance in culture may generate a score similar to this:

Process x Culture = Mediocre Results
3   x   7   =   21

Obviously, such an organization would be lopsided in the reverse. This organization should focus on shoring up its process hemisphere. Undertaking a pervasive improvement program—documenting, measuring, and streamlining the organization's system of work—would eventually bring the two hemispheres into balance, delivering a much greater yield. The resulting outcome might be similar to the experience described below:

Process x Culture = Approaching Breakpoint
7   x   7   =   49

But what happens to organizations who *do* try to operate with half a brain—favoring their dominant hemisphere only? Ironically, this strategy actually makes things worse! The more one hemisphere is emphasized over the other, the worse the performance in the complementary dimension. To illustrate, let's go back to our original equation:

Process x Culture = Mediocre Results
7   x   3   =   21

Emphasizing process further may raise this bar incrementally (it becomes more difficult as you travel higher up the scale). But doing so without energized and involved people will give rise to even more inflexible structures and reduced cooperation, almost certainly serving to *lower* performance in the cultural dimension. This would very likely turn a poor culture into a *terrible* culture. The result would no doubt look something like this:

Improved Process x Diminished Culture = Even Worse Results!
8   x   2   =   16

The key to Superperformance is balance, operating with the full mutual expression of process and culture. After bringing the hemispheres into balance, the task is simple—continued emphasis on both process and culture together.

PROCESS	CULTURE	PREDICTED RESULTS
LOW	LOW	POOR
LOW	HIGH	MEDIOCRE
HIGH	LOW	MEDIOCRE
HIGH	HIGH	SUPER

Why the Formula Works

When we begin to think of an organization as a living system, we notice that process and culture operate according to the same principles as our own brains. It is a well-known fact that our brains are divided into

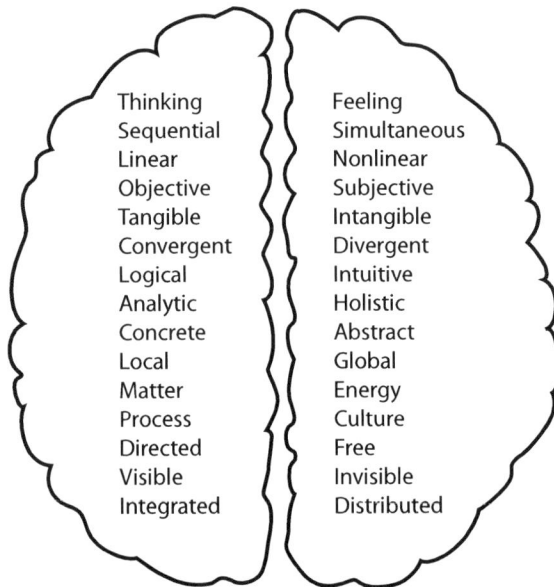

Thinking	Feeling
Sequential	Simultaneous
Linear	Nonlinear
Objective	Subjective
Tangible	Intangible
Convergent	Divergent
Logical	Intuitive
Analytic	Holistic
Concrete	Abstract
Local	Global
Matter	Energy
Process	Culture
Directed	Free
Visible	Invisible
Integrated	Distributed

Brain functions in two hemispheres.

two distinct hemispheres and that each side has separate processing and intuiting tasks. The left-brain is primarily verbal, orienting to sequential, mathematical patterns, while the right-brain is primarily nonverbal, orienting to parallel, holistic patterns. The two hemispheres are distinctly different, controlling different functions. But they still operate together, each lobe requiring the other for wholeness and completion.[1]

Somewhat more obscure is the high-leverage intersection between the hemispheres, in the part of the brain known as the corpus callosum. The corpus callosum is the connecting terminal between the two lobes, the main channel between the two hemispheres, consisting of a profuse number of neural connections. It is a large bundle of more than 200 million nerve fibers that radiate throughout as well as join the two hemispheres of the brain. The corpus callosum allows the two lobes to communicate with each other. It holds the most complex group of nerves in the human body and provides for an integrated whole brain—and consciousness.[2]

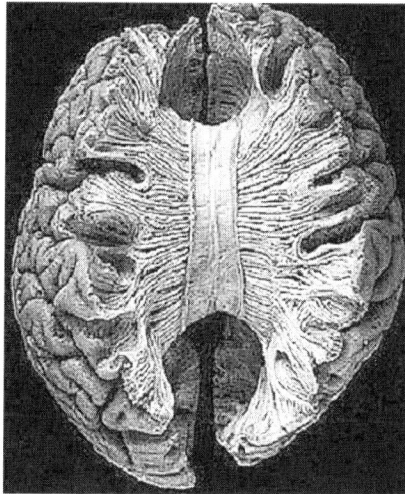

The Corpus Callosum radiates throughout both hemispheres.
(Photo. The Virtual Hospital, University of Iowa.)

It is through the neural connections of the corpus callosum that the two hemispheres work together for wholeness. Superperforming process and culture interconnect in precisely the same way. It is only through the full expression of this core partnership that organizations become everything they can be.

Polar-Complementarity

Organizations share this foundation of opposites with all of life in general. We inhabit a universe of chaos and order, left and right, male and female, expand and contract. Every day we buy and sell, twist and turn, think and feel. Wherever you look, life organizes as *polar-complements*.

The ancient Chinese philosophy

"Rabbit's clever," said Pooh thoughtfully.
"Yes," said Piglet, "Rabbit's clever."
"And he has Brain."
"Yes," said Pooh, "Rabbit has brain."
There was a long silence.
"I suppose," said Pooh, "that that's why he never understands anything."

THE HOUSE ON POOH CORNER

of yin-yang holds that everything in nature consists of opposite forces, which must remain in balance for life to thrive. The yin and yang are opposing forces that constantly shift, operating in continual conflict, yet at the same time requiring each other for completion. These opposites drive each other toward creativity and excellence, while simultaneously restraining each other to inspire harmony. To the ancient Chinese, there was nothing in life that was exempt from the pervasive influence of yin-yang.[3]

Chinese Yin-Yang Symbol.

Twenty-first-century physicists exploring the immutable forces of nature have come to the same conclusion. In referring to this inescapable influence, Nobel Physicist Niels Bohr's famous *complementarity principle* described the paradox of the particle-wave duality encountered at the subatomic level of light. Bohr discovered that light fundamentally consists of streams of particles (photons) that also paradoxically behave like waves.[4]

Later, Bohr saw evidence of complementarity everywhere. He predicted that knowledge of complementarity and its omnipresent influence would one day become the common knowledge of schoolchildren. Not just subatomic particles, but all of reality, he insisted, fall under its sway: "We have been forced to recognize that we must modify not only all our concepts of classical physics but even the ideas we use in everyday life."[5] This revelation led to Bohr's famous choice of inscription on the Bohr family coat of arms: *Contraria sunt Complementa* (Latin for "Opposites are Complements").[6]

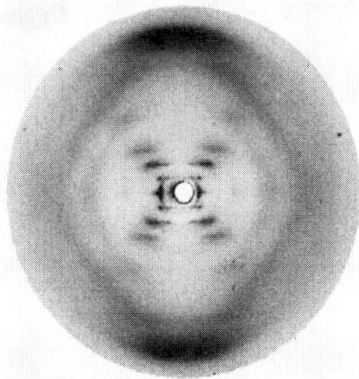

Rosalind Franklin's Photo 51.
(Photo: Cold Spring Harbor Laboratory Archives.)

In Biology, polar-complementarity appears in the double helix of DNA. Rosalind Franklin's famous purloined *Photo 51* revealed to James Watson the double helix structure of the DNA molecule. "The instant I saw the picture my mouth fell open and my heart began to race,"

Watson later reported.[7] *Photo 51* resembled a fuzzy "X," whose diffracted image translated the DNA molecule for Watson into a double-helix shape. Soon after, Watson's collaborator Francis Crick read a report containing Rosalind Franklin's recent measurements of the DNA molecule. Immediately upon confirming Franklin's correlating numbers, Crick knew they had identified the "secret of life."[8] Crick and Watson concluded that the DNA molecule was indeed made of two strands—a double helix—running in opposite directions. The blueprint for life is made of complementary bases and twisted pairs. In a word, opposites.

> # The Toyota Way, along with the Toyota Production System, make up Toyota's DNA.
>
> GARY CONVIS, PRESIDENT, TOYOTA NORTH AMERICA

In Psychology Jung found the introvert/extrovert and thinking/feeling opposites.[9]

In Mathematics we have positive and negative, linear and nonlinear descriptions—opposites again!

Even in the Digital world, in binary language, we write code from a foundation of 1s and 0s.

Edge of Chaos

Yet another exciting, crucial image for understanding Superperformance comes from complexity science. The "Edge of Chaos," a term coined by computer scientist Chris Langton of the Santa Fe Institute, describes the crest of "optimum fitness," a point balanced precariously at the border between just enough chaos and just enough order. The edge of chaos is a permeable, center region through which order and disorder flow. Moving closer to the edge of chaos will create great disequilibrium but not dispersion.[10]

According to scientists who study this region, all of life self-organizes, or advances, toward this state. In organizations, the edge of chaos is more of a dynamic, persistent condition than it is a location. Navigating in this space is surfing the edge of chaos—and order. This continuously shifting border is an inexorable point of attraction for optimum fitness. Complexity scientists report that it is here that living systems are their most robust,

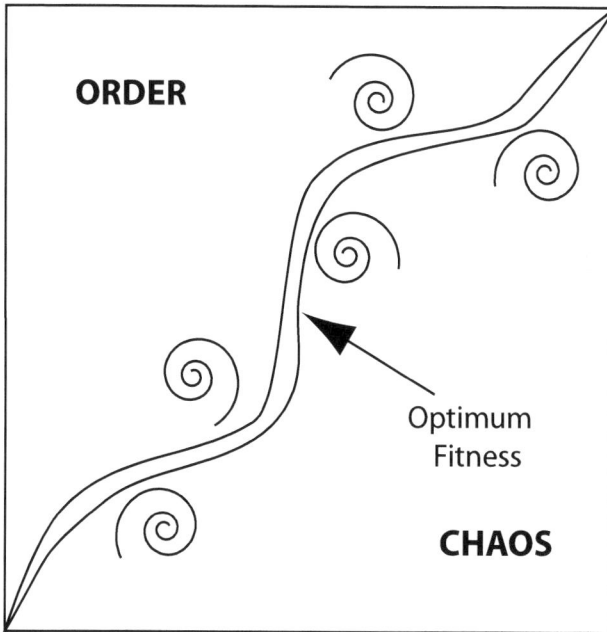

"The Edge of Chaos," adapted from Welsh (1996).

containing the greatest potential for adaptability and learning. Here an organism is "maximally responsive to the variety in its environment but sufficiently structured so that it can act and perpetuate itself."[11]

Successfully surfing the edge of chaos calls for finding the exact point between too much and not enough change—or stability.

In Superperforming organizations, the edge of chaos maximizes the interaction of process and culture. That's why this image is so central to a complete understanding of Superperformance. Organizations and other living systems operate at their best near the edge of chaos.

The edge of chaos is not the brink of oblivion; it is the sweet spot of Superperformance.

Another idea to keep in mind, though, is that an organization's

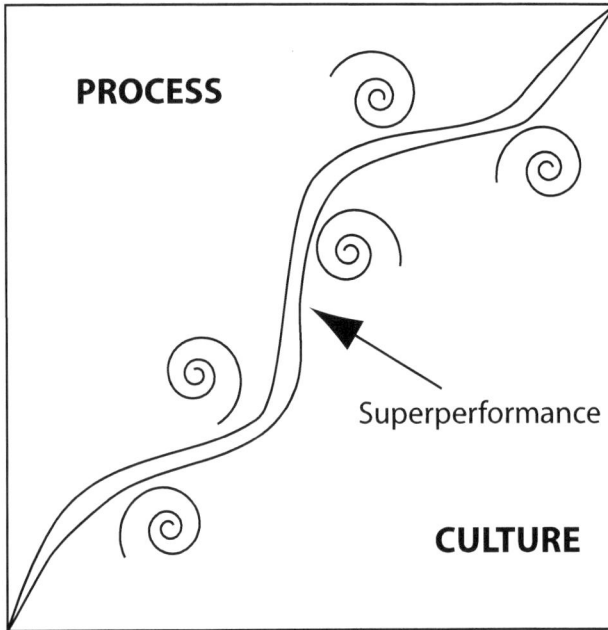

The Sweet Spot of Superperformance.

particular fitness landscape is constantly changing in response to outside influences. The edge of chaos isn't static; it's an ever-emerging wave that an organization, to successfully co-evolve with its environment, must ride continuously.

Superperforming companies leverage this same ubiquitous relationship. It is this interaction that powers the phase transition to Superperformance explored further in Chapter 7. It is also the meaning of Southwest Airlines' Chairman and former CEO Herb Kelleher's profound assertion, "Anyone who thinks of business only in terms of the visible numbers is missing the heart of business, which is people."

Superperformers like Southwest Airlines have simply married their tangible and intangible parts to escape to a new level—Superperformance.

Summary

- Superperformance is defined as industry-outperforming return on investment sustained over time. Only a few organizations qualify as Superperformers.

- Superperformance is distinguishable from flash performance, defined as short-term outperformance driven by expedience.

- The Superperformance Formula (Process x Culture = Superperformance) is at work in every instance of organizational Superperformance.

- The Superperformance Formula works because process and culture are *polar-complements*, opposing but also in need of each other for completion. These dimensions work in organizations the same way our own left and right brains work.

- Organizations share this foundation of opposites with all of nature.

- Organizational Superperformance emerges at the edge of chaos, the location of "optimum fitness" in all living systems.

8 Simple Rules

RULE 1:   Process x Culture = Superperformance

RULE 2:   Superperformers superperform over time

Chapter 2

The Business End of Superperformance

The Superperformers

You wouldn't want to take on any of these companies in a fight to the finish. They are miraculous—absolutely *transcendent*—in the levels of performance they are able to achieve and sustain. They operate in a different stratosphere, in a different steady state from their industry peers. And what's more, they make it look easy. They are the marvels of free-enterprise—far and away the best in the business. Together, they operate in the *Zone of Superperformance*, in a position of industry outperformance across much of our economy.

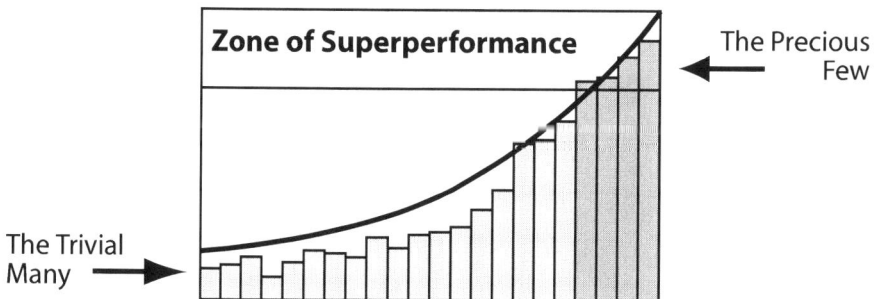

Who are these amazing companies, and what are their stories? What are their behaviors, their habits?

They are incredibly resilient, with a minimum of a dozen years of unbroken industry outperformance. This is an astonishing feat. When durability is considered, very few companies can be identified as true Superperformers.

RULE 2: Superperformers Superperform Over Time

Superperformers generate *sustainable* industry-outperforming return on investment. They demonstrate operational excellence and not only satisfy but thrill their customers. They are powered by wholly engaged and committed people. They enjoy comparatively higher valuations and publicly trade at dramatically higher price to earnings (PE) ratios than their industry peers.

Their brands are globally recognized for the highest quality and singular long-term value. Based on this lofty criteria, following are ten organizational Superperformers:

Superperformer	Industry
Berkshire Hathaway	Capital Investment
Harley Davidson	Motorcycles
Johnson & Johnson	Healthcare Products
Microsoft	Software
Southwest Airlines	Airlines
Sterling Bancshares	Regional Banking
SYSCO	Food Distribution
Tiffany & Company	Jewelry
Toyota	Automobiles
Wal-Mart	Retailing

Economic Superforce

As a group, they are an economic superforce. Investing $25,000 in a hypothetical "Superperformance Fund" equally divided between these ten companies twenty years ago, allowing for the late arrival of Tiffany & Co. (1987), Harley Davidson (1987), SYSCO (1987), and Sterling Bancshares (1992), would pay back a stunning $1.4 million today! Even though much of this gain is contributed by Microsoft, each of these ten companies outperformed their industries for the entire period, creating a dramatically greater return on investment. As a group they produced an average annual rate of return of 22%, and a rate of return for the entire period of well over 5680%.

$25,000 Investment in Superperformance vs S&P 500

Comparative Returns 20 Years (1985 to 2005)	S&P 500 Mnthly Reinv	Hypothetical Superperformance Fund
Annual Rate of Return	12.2%	22%
Cumulative Rate of Return	912%	5680%
Twenty Year Actual Return	$228,000	$1,400,000

Constructed courtesy AIM Investments and Morningstar.com.

While they are unmistakable long-term outperformers, even in the short term Superperformers show signs of greatness. A hypothetical $25,000 invested in this same fund just ten years ago, in 1995, would be worth in excess of $130,000 today (a cumulative rate of return of over 420%)—outstanding short-term performance when compared to the performance of mutual funds in existence today.

21

The economic achievement of these ten companies validates the awesome power of the Superperformance formula (PxC=SP). A close study of their behavior reveals an amplified interaction of process and culture in every case.

Each Superperformer has elevated its core business model to an art form. They have all evolved unique adaptations that stand out in their particular fitness landscapes as extraordinary advantages. Take Wal-Mart's famous distribution system, for example. Or the miraculously efficient Toyota Production System. Or Harley Davidson's cult-level branding. The pattern of Superperformance is always the same. Always there is some super-evolved, adaptive advantage.

Any Organization Can Become a Superperformer

The evidence of these super results, when we view organizations as organisms (rather than machines), points to a simpler model and a new road map to optimization from anywhere. Using this paradigm, any organization can make the shift to Superperformance.

By no means does the experience of these ten companies capture all of organizational Superperformance. These represent major segments of the economy: software, airlines, retailing, automobiles, healthcare products, and several others. But they are certainly not a complete list. Superperformance can be found alive and well in many other areas, including the not-for-profit sector, healthcare, government, education, and the small enterprise realm. Often a Superperformer is an outperforming unit inside an otherwise mechanistically mired parent system. But wherever you find it, Superperformance yields the same delicious fruit: transcendent operating performance; spectacular business process and culture; and a deep, unmistakable propensity for the long view.

Returning to our ten Superperformers; here are their stories:

Berkshire Hathaway: Capital Investing

Superfacts:

- As of January 2005 Berkshire Hathaway held $43 billion in cash.

- Berkshire Hathaway has never split its stock. The price of a share in the company in 1982 was $750. As of mid-year 2005, one share is worth $84,400.

- Not one Berkshire Hathaway CEO has left the company to work for someone else in 38 years.

- The oldest Berkshire manager was Rose Blumkin (102) of Nebraska Furniture Mart.

- Anyone can learn from Warren Buffett by visiting Berkshire Hathaway's web site (www.berkshirehathaway.com) and reading Warren Buffett's and Charlie Mungers' letters to shareholders. In addition Berkshire Hathaway published an *Owners Manual* in 1996, outlining its "Owner-Related Business Principles."

- More than 99% of Warren Buffett's net worth is vested in Berkshire Hathaway stock.

Superstory

Warren Buffett is the superhero of value investors. His investment strategies and management techniques are widely sought-after and hungrily devoured by business people, investors, and Wall Street pundits everywhere. Buffett and his partner Charlie Munger have grown Berkshire Hathaway into a multi-billion dollar empire, made up of over 100 wholly owned subsidiaries and a portfolio of partly owned common stocks. Its holdings include significant property and casualty insurance businesses, cash, and fixed-income investments.

Originally a textile manufacturer, the company has become an investment and holding company operated by Buffett and Munger in a remarkably spartan home office (its staff numbers less than 20 employees) based in Omaha, Nebraska. Much of the Berkshire Hathaway story is already legendary, from Buffett's fondness for cash-generating insurance companies and his hands-off managerial style, to his early embrace of the security analysis principles of value-investing guru Benjamin Graham. But from the perspective of Process x Culture, Berkshire Hathaway's story is especially illuminating.

Berkshire Hathaway, with 172,000 employees, is a Superperformer made up of Superperformers. The company owns a myriad of stellar companies, including some well-known brands like GEICO Insurance, Sees Candy Shops, General Re, Benjamin Moore Paints, Fruit of the Loom, and Dairy Queen, as well as many lesser known but likewise extraordinary companies like Acme Brick Company, Larson-Juhl Custom Frames, CTB Food and Grain, and Garan Children's Clothing.

> Our favorite holding period is forever.
>
> WARREN BUFFETT

Its acquisition policy—buying excellent owner-operated businesses and enticing owners to stay—has been core. Take, for example, the case of Nebraska Furniture Mart, operated by 102-year-old centenarian and founder Rose Blumkin (Mrs. B) and the Blumkin family. Russian immigrant Rose Blumkin founded The Furniture Mart in 1937 in a basement shop with the motto, "Sell cheap and tell the truth." The Furniture Mart grew into a colossus, with Rose and her family working long hours every day. Under Mrs. B's guidance, The Furniture Mart grew into a Nebraska legend. The original 3000-square-foot store today occupies 75 acres.

As a local resident, Warren Buffett knew about The Furniture Mart and the wonderful business it had become. According to the story, Buffett walked into the store one day, approached Mrs. B, and asked her if she wanted to sell and, if so, to name her price. Mrs B declared that she was a seller at $60 million, and Buffett accepted immediately. He insisted, though, on Rose and her sons, by then helping her to run the business, retaining a minority share and continuing to manage the business.

Buffett knew from previous inquiries that the business was grossing about $15 million a year in profits, but seemed to have done little additional checking, settling the deal within a few days, without audits or due diligence. He knew a good deal when he saw it, and, as he was later to say, he trusted her integrity.[1]

Besides its owned subsidiaries, Berkshire Hathaway also has highly profitable permanent holdings in such companies as Coca Cola, Gillette, American Express, and The Washington Post.

Berkshire Hathaway does not pay dividends, although management has allowed that dividends may be paid at some later date.[2]

Buffett is a mathematical whiz with a phenomenal grasp for numbers. In the early years of his investing career, he successfully turned this prodigious talent to a form of investing he termed "cigar butt" investing: "Finding a business with a last puff remaining and then extracting the 'pure' profit from that single puff."[3] But cigar butts are not very satisfying. Buffet described his slow but certain conversion

> A little unlearning goes a long way.
>
> Richard Kehl

from only quantitative investing to combining quantitative with qualitative considerations. He changed from buying fair companies at a great price to buying great companies at a fair price. He credited Charlie Munger as the influence that brought him to this awareness:

> Charlie said, let's go for the wonderful business. We both realized that time is the friend of the wonderful business and the enemy of the mediocre. You might think this principle is obvious, but I had to learn it the hard way. In fact, I had to learn it several times over.
>
> It's far better to buy a wonderful company at a fair price than a fair company at a wonderful price. Charlie Munger understood this early; I was a slow learner. Now, when buying companies or common stocks, we look for first-class businesses accompanied by first-class managements.[4]

Buffett already had the mathematical tools and brilliant insight for determining the intrinsic value (predicted future cash flows compared to current price) of a potential acquisition. But Charlie Munger preached that intrinsic value also included a company's psychology—and that this colored the durability of its earnings potential. And a large part of company psychology is influenced by corporate culture and management's ingenuity, service, brand, marketing, and managerial competence—in essence, management's ability to *create* value. Above all, Munger encouraged Buffett to look for value in management's capacity

> "You know Wall Street," Warren tried to reassure me, "People don't think in a long-term way there."
>
> KATHERINE GRAHAM IN PERSONAL HISTORY

to "act like an owner," then to invest in these good businesses at a fair price. Today both dimensions figure prominently in Berkshire Hathaway's evaluation of potential acquisitions. This has made Berkshire Hathaway not only an acquirer of Superperformers, but possibly the world's only *Superperformance conglomerate*.

Although there is a deep ocean of knowledge, wisdom, and experience underlying Berkshire's formidable capabilities, the company's core process mastery is greatly illuminated in two areas: (1) Managing Capital and (2) Leading People. Captured well in the book, *The Real Warren Buffet*, by James O'Loughlin, these polar-complements are at the core of Berkshire Hathaway's amazing long-term outperformance.[5]

As for corporate culture, Berkshire Hathaway's unconventional approach to motivating its managers is especially instructive and refreshing. Buffett is notoriously hands-off when it comes to managing Berkshire Hathaway's subsidiaries (they are already great), but he is always available to Berkshire Hathaway's top managers to offer counsel and encouragement. As Sees Candy CEO Chuck Huggins reflects,

> He's always available, and that's really remarkable. So I don't feel that
> I am his employee, or a provider of things that he wants his company
> to do, but that I am also his friend and confidant. Right from the

beginning and ever since, he has treated me as a partner and an equal.[6]

Buffett's only request of his CEOs is that they run their companies as if they are the sole asset of their families and will remain so for the next century.

Buffett, an analytical genius, has a fundamental respect for people, as well as an intuitive grasp for the power of intrinsic motivation. "I found in running businesses that the best results come from letting high-grade people work unencumbered," he says.[7] Buffett's rules are minimal, designed to motivate and encourage a manager to act like an owner. Charlie Munger adds:

> There are certain virtues that are common in all of Berkshire's subsidiaries. We don't create them—we select companies that have them already. We just don't screw it up....There's a lot of human love in building at least some businesses and some people who own businesses love them. They don't want to sell to a financial buyer who will dress it up and strip it down. When we buy a company, we don't tinker with winning businesses. So, for some sellers, ... Berkshire Hathaway was the only acceptable buyer. If you want a culture like ours, I don't know anywhere to get it if not here.[8]

Harley-Davidson: Motorcycles

Superfacts:

- The Harley Owners Group® (HOG) numbering 900,000 members worldwide, celebrated its 22nd anniversary in 2005.

- In 2004, Harley-Davidson recorded its nineteenth consecutive year of record revenue and earnings.

- Harley-Davidson has made *Fortune's* list of "100 Best Companies to Work For" for seven out of the last eight years.

- Harley-Davidson owners raised a record-shattering $7,200,000 for the Muscular Dystrophy Association in 2003.

- Harley-Davidson celebrated its 100th anniversary throughout 2002. Over 1,000,000 people participated in celebration events in 47 countries.

Superstory

Harley-Davidson is as iconic as James Dean, Clark Gable, Marlon Brando, and Elvis Presley. All of these Hollywood super rebels have straddled Harleys. This famous brand evokes images of sleek styling, black-leather-clad easyriders, and get-away-from-it-all open-road cruising.

A spry 100 years old in 2003, Harley-Davidson has hit a few potholes in its time, overcoming the automobile, the Great Depression, two World Wars, and Japanese quality to become the world leader in heavyweight motorcycles. The company's early rise came from supplying the US Military with motorcycles during World War II.

> Every blade of grass has an angel that bends over it and whispers, "Grow, grow."
>
> THE TALMUD

After the war Harley-Davidson increased its recreational identity, introducing a steady stream of motorcycles, including the K-Model (which evolved into the Sportster), Duo-Glide, Sprint, Electra-Glide, and others. On a parallel track, the company was going into reverse—experiencing sliding revenues and declining product quality. By 1979 the company was acquired by American Machines and Foundry (AMF), who put the company up for sale a few years later in even worse operating condition than before the merger.

In 1981, in classic Superhero style, thirteen managers risked everything to purchase the sputtering company in a leveraged buyout. Afterwards the company fought to regain market share, which had dropped to 13% by 1983, placing it on the brink of bankruptcy. Richard Teerlink was part of a seven-person Policy Committee formed to redevelop the operating and financial strategies of the company. Under Teerlink's leadership, Harley-Davidson's new owner-managers recognized that the company would have to undergo a complete metamorphosis to survive. Deep analysis of the company's problems uncovered the following:

- Corporate management had been focused primarily on the short-term.
- Management did not listen to employees or give them ownership for quality.
- High parts inventories consumed cash and reduced productivity.
- The threat of foreign competition had been miscalculated.

Harley-Davidson's new owner-managers focused on addressing these crucial flaws and regaining lost share from the Japanese. Teerlink, a Deming disciple, led the transformation. He describes the challenge as, "Getting leaders to believe that we needed to reinvent the company and recognizing that we—the leaders—were the problem." The company instituted new quality methods, including Just-In-Time (JIT) production, organization-wide continual improvement, and statistical process control.

At the same time, Harley-Davidson reinvented its culture, from top-down management to a company of complete and total employee involvement. The most vivid example was the rare relationship the company forged with its union. Harley

> Leadership is a process in which we bring people together to work toward mutual goals because they want to, not because they have to.
>
> RICHARD TEERLINK

Davidson's consistent good-faith dealings transformed the union into a true partner. Bob Klebar, president of the union at the time, characterized this approach as union working closely with production, and everyone concentrating on the final customer: "It really binds us together and makes us go in the right direction."[9] According to Teerlink, "Total employee involvement cannot exist until management and labor can agree that they have a mutual goal: the long-term success of the company."[10]

The changes took, and Harley-Davidson has come roaring back. Since its initial public offering in 1986, Harley-Davidson has posted record sales and earnings every year. It has improved quality and reliability consistently, overtaking every other competitor, including the formidable Japanese, to win back US and global market share.

In describing the impact to the famous Harley-Davidson brand, Teerlink mused:

> In our case, we found that it was necessary to start with the basics. Fix the product so that it had high quality and reliability. To do this we had to improve quality in our manufacturing process and then develop new products with higher levels of quality and reliability built in from the start. Then we had to show the customer that we had products that worked. In that way, we changed the brand promise. By changing the brand promise you also created competitive advantage.[11]

Johnson & Johnson: Healthcare Products

Superfacts

- In 2005 Johnson & Johnson employed over 110,000 people in 57 countries.

- Johnson & Johnson posted 2004 sales of $47 billion, with net income growth of 18%.

- Many Johnson & Johnson products, such as Band-Aid®, Johnson Baby Powder®, and Tylenol® are globally recognized brands used in over 175 countries.

- In 1982 the company weathered a $240 million product recall spurred by the deaths of eight people who took Tylenol capsules laced with cyanide. The company's exemplary quick response to this crisis cemented its reputation as the most ethical company in America.

- Johnson & Johnson remains one of a handful of companies with a triple-A credit rating, thanks to its pristine balance sheet.

- Since 1943 Johnson & Johnson has been guided by its credo, a one-page statement of purpose originally developed by Robert Wood Johnson. The credo describes Johnson & Johnson's responsibility to its customers, employees, the community and stockholders.

Superstory

Johnson & Johnson, with approximately 110,000 employees, is the world's most comprehensive, broadly based producer of health care products, serving three markets: consumers, medical devices and diagnostics, and pharmaceuticals. Founded in 1886 by James and Edward Johnson, the company's first product success was a surgical dressing developed by a third Johnson brother, Robert. The company introduced its famous Band-Aid adhesive bandages in 1921, participating as a pioneer in the health care industry. In the 1930s, Johnson & Johnson decentralized, which provided autonomy to the growing family of Johnson & Johnson companies. The decentralization practice continues today to drive innovation within Johnson & Johnson's 200+ operating divisions.

> We believe the first responsibility of business is to its customers.
>
> FROM JOHNSON & JOHNSON CREDO

As might be expected of a company whose products deal with child and health care, Johnson & Johnson is described as having a "very family friendly" culture. "It is a great company to work for," says one insider, and another concurs that there are "good benefits, great employee perks, and a conscious responsibility to the community." Among its family-friendly perks are more on-site childcare centers than any other company, $3,000 reimbursement for adoption expenses, a 75% match of up to 6% of salary for its 401(k) program, and even a health and wellness plan.

Organic growth and resilience take on new meaning at Johnson & Johnson. In April 2002, Bill Weldon took the reins from Ralph Larsen, who had led the company through more than a decade of double-digit growth. Weldon is only the sixth chairman in Johnson & Johnson's 117-year history. Weldon started his Johnson & Johnson career as a sales representative out of college. The company Weldon inherited from his predecessor had already been a consistent industry-outperformer for decades.

Much of Johnson & Johnson's success has hinged on its unique culture and decentralized structure. Up to now, Johnson & Johnson's far-flung units have operated pretty much as independent enterprises, each with its own strategy, human resources department, etc. Johnson & Johnson has been able to turn itself into a healthcare powerhouse precisely because the businesses it buys, and the ones it starts, are given near total autonomy.

> Life has an overall purpose. Men must judge their conduct, not merely in terms of personal gain or convenience, but also as right or wrong.
>
> ROBERT WOOD JOHNSON

That independence fosters an entrepreneurial attitude that has kept Johnson & Johnson intensely competitive as others around it have faltered.

However, the medical industry landscape is changing. New genomic testing could determine who will respond to a certain cancer drug; sutures and implants are now coated with antibiotics; defibrillators can be linked to computers and alert doctors when patients have abnormal heart rhythms. The treatment of many diseases is becoming vastly more sophisticated. Johnson & Johnson is positioned to take advantage of this trend toward the convergence of medical devices, diagnostics, and pharmaceuticals. Few companies have all these divisions under one roof. But Johnson & Johnson can cash in only if its fiercely independent businesses can work together in a new way. The odds are in Johnson & Johnson's favor that they will.

Microsoft: Software

Superfacts

- In 2005 Microsoft's stock market capitalization reached $274 billion.

- Microsoft carries $71 billion in cash and investments on its balance sheet and generates enormous operating cash flow and free cash flow.

- In 2005 Microsoft made Fortune's "100 Best Companies to Work For" list for the eighth year in a row, marking a place on the list every year since its inception.

- In 2004 the company announced a plan to return $75 billion to shareholders through dividends and stock repurchases.

- Microsoft compensation and benefits are described by many as the best in the industry.

- The Bill and Melinda Gates Foundation, with an endowment of $26 billion, is the world's largest private giver. It has donated over $4 billion since its start in 1996, and focuses on improving healthcare and education for children around the world.

Superstory

Microsoft is the global leviathan of business and consumer software, furnishing the operating system and core business software for most PCs used in the world. Microsoft provides a variety of products and services, including its Windows operating systems and Office software suite. Today Microsoft is the dominant force in almost every major software category.

Although some would argue that Microsoft's super growth years are behind it, the company is still an amazing cash-generating phenomenon. Microsoft's many new business initiatives have garnered a lot of attention over the past several years; but even so, more than 60% of the company's revenue (and virtually all of its profits) comes from core businesses—the Microsoft Windows operating system and the Microsoft Office line of desktop applications. These two businesses respectively produce operating margins of 81% and 76%, and those margins are not in jeopardy.

The company understands the importance of referencing the core while building new businesses. To that end, it has devoted over 21% of revenue to research and development—over $7.7 billion in 2004.

Microsoft is consistently listed in Fortune's "100 Best Companies to Work For" survey in the US and Europe. "It's a great company," says Anna Pringle, Microsoft Ireland Human Resources Director. "It's a successful company and Microsoft has become great by treating people well." She adds,

> One of the key tenets here is that it is a great company with great values, and one of those values is respect for one another. That plays out through a willingness to listen to employee feedback. We conduct an annual survey, called the MS Poll, across the organization and managers take it very seriously as it affects how managers are perceived. Action plans are based on the results of the survey in order to improve scores the following year.[12]

Respect for the individual is demonstrated in other ways. These include openness between leaders and employees. "It is not unusual for people to receive emails directly from Bill Gates or Steve Ballmer, our CEO," says Pringle. "And it's not unheard of for people to send emails to Bill or Steve directly."

Day-to-day, this informal approach shows up as no executive parking places and an internal telephone directory that is organized on a first-name basis. "People talk about Steve B and Bill G," says Pringle.

> I'm Anna P while the head of HR in Washington is Ken D. We also have a great cafeteria. Everybody goes there and there are long tables with lots of people chatting. There's no executive cafeteria. There may be people in senior management who travel more or who have outside

responsibilities, but the dress code is very casual and you can't tell by looking at someone what their status is.[13]

David Thielen's interesting and informative *The 12 Simple Secrets of Microsoft Management* examines Microsoft's entrepreneurial culture. Software development, marketing and planning teams are all focused on a common goal: winning 100% of their target market, in whatever category. Microsoft's overarching focus is one of maximizing long-term profits by capturing market share in strategic markets.[14]

No doubt about it, the scourge of most large organizations is bureaucracy with dumb rules. Rules at Microsoft are few, and the ones that do exist usually make sense. Having only a few important rules assures that people will actually remember and follow them.

Microsoft uses different methods to maximize productivity. Besides the fabled Microsoft employee stock options, the company allows every person's office to be individualized, creating more of an at-home atmosphere.

> ## Securities analysts continue to get it wrong. Companies don't make money. They make shoes.
>
> PETER DRUCKER

Everything values individuality—true offices (no cubicles), with windows in most offices, free soft drinks, no dress code, an open supply room, and anytime work hours. These and other similar practices energize employee morale and increase overall productivity. Microsoft associates take great pride in the company, in part because they are given great freedom in how they go about their jobs.

The company also makes a conscious effort to ensure there is work/life balance. The nature of the software business means that people must make sacrifices to ensure that products ship on time and that the company acknowledges this through various programs. "People can take up to three months leave of absence," explains Pringle. "There is also flexibility in the hours people work. We also help employees get broadband installed at home so there is also a degree of flexibility in where they work."[15]

Like many large companies, Microsoft offers health insurance. It also provides ad-hoc services such as a chair massage or *reiki*. They offer workshops in stress management and, of course, throw parties to celebrate making deadlines. And, to acknowledge the sacrifices family members make, there are family days.

The particular needs of women are recognized. There is an Annual Women's Conference held in the US which Steve Ballmer and other senior executives attend. Women from all over the Microsoft organization participate in roundtable discussions on a range of issues relating to the needs of working mothers, and this participant feedback finds its way into the design of policies and processes.

While theories abound to explain Microsoft's success, a few fundamental strategies have been paramount: hire the best and the brightest; reward their allegiance with lucrative stock options; foster an egalitarian, creative work atmosphere; and perpetuate the identity of small working groups.

Southwest Airlines: Airlines

Superfacts

- As of 2005, Southwest has enjoyed 32 consecutive years of profitability.

- For the ninth year in a row, *Fortune* has recognized Southwest Airlines among America's most admired corporations. In 2005, for the tenth year in a row, Southwest also was named most admired airline.

- Southwest has ranked number one in fewest Customer complaints for the last 14 consecutive years as published in the Department of Transportation's "Air Travel Consumer Report."

- The airline began the first profit-sharing plan in the US airline industry in 1974. Through the plan, employees own at least 10% of the Company stock.

- Southwest received 225,895 resumes and hired 1,706 new Employees in 2004.

- The "Triple Crown Award" was created by the company to highlight the fact that Southwest has the best performance in three key service areas: on-time record, baggage handling, and fewest customer complaints—an amazing, blistering, "Seabiscuit of a performance."

- *Fortune Magazine* recently described Chairman and former CEO Herb Kelleher as perhaps America's Best CEO ever.

Superstory

As the airline industry maverick, Southwest Airlines is the poster child for organizational Superperformance. Southwest has outperformed its entire class, consistently, for three decades. It flies only Boeing 737s for fuel efficiency, safety, and cost. And it flies them better than anyone else in the world. Passengers may sit anywhere they like— seating is first-come, first serve. Southwest

> Love is metaphysical gravity.
>
> R. BUCKMINSTER FULLER

culture is legendary—from a stock symbol of LUV, to the folksy humor that characterizes the Southwest Airlines flight experience.

But make no mistake about it—Southwest is a process champion too. Southwest is the only airline in the world capable of turning an airplane around in fifteen minutes. It does it with fewer people too. The company has won the "Triple Crown" of service—on-time performance, flawless baggage handling, and fewest customer complaints—for five astounding years in a row.

Southwest is a master of sticking to what works, having taken a simple business model and refined it to a breathtaking polish. The company has been highly successful expanding its economical, no-frills approach throughout the US to serve over 60 cities in 30 states. Southwest offers ticketless travel and operates its own reservation system. The company has enjoyed 32 consecutively profitable years, a phenomenal performance given the comparable performance of the entire airline industry.

Southwest Airlines Chairman and former CEO Herb Kelleher, in a recent *Fortune Magazine* interview, in response to the question, "What keeps you up at night (regarding the future of Southwest Airlines)?" reflected:

> What keeps me awake are the intangibles. It's the intangibles that are the hardest thing for a competitor to imitate. You can get airplanes, you can get ticket counter space, you can get tugs, you can get baggage conveyers. But the spirit of Southwest is the most difficult thing to emulate. So my biggest concern is that somehow, through maladroitness, through inattention, through misunderstanding, we lose the *esprit de corps*, the culture, the spirit. If we ever do lose that, we will have lost our most valuable competitive asset.[16]

Superperformers like Southwest Airlines are mystified by a business world that remains stubbornly tethered to Machine View. In the final pages of Kevin and Jackie Freiberg's wonderfully entertaining and authoritative book about Southwest Airlines, the authors bemoan this continuing preoccupation with process over culture: "In doing the research for *NUTS!* it wasn't surprising to see

> We hire leaders for every position. Leadership has nothing to do with title.
>
> Colleen Barrett

that the overwhelming majority of articles in the business press focus on the operations of Southwest Airlines, not on the spirit of its people."[17]

Even though Southwest Airlines can boast profoundly superior operating performance, the cultural component is what the company counts as its secret to success.

Sterling Bancshares: Regional Banking

Superfacts

- Sterling, a Texas-based "Supercommunity" banking system, has realized 1000 fold growth in 30 years, going from $3 million to over $3 billion in assets.

- In 2005, Sterling was recognized for the third year in a row in *Fortune's* "100 Best Companies to Work For" annual survey.

- Every Sterling employee holds the title of "Sterling Banker."

- Sterling bankers enjoy generous employee stock options, compensation and benefits that average a significant 18.5% higher than commercial banks, plus over 54 hours of development per year.

- Sterling has transformed its tellers into "front-line managers" supported by professional training at Sterling University.

Superstory

Sterling's luster is hard to ignore. Sterling Bancshares is the holding company for Sterling Bank, which provides commercial and retail banking services through almost forty offices in the Houston, Dallas, and San Antonio area. As with many Superperformers, Sterling goes where no competitor has gone before. Sterling discovered its sweet spot early on and is tenacious about staying in it: ultra-servicing the small-business banking customer. While small business customers usually represent a greater credit risk, Sterling's portfolio of over 20,000 loans spread across many different industries shows otherwise. According to George Martinez, founder and former CEO and Chairman, the larger risk would be to move away from Sterling's finely tuned business model.

> We have learned how important it is to stay in our sweet spot. It's very seductive for banks, especially large banks, to try to be all things to all people—grow the portfolio of large corporate customers, retail

consumers, and small businesses combined—this only dilutes any niche strength a bank may have, and increases the odds of under-performing at all three.[18]

Sterling lives its beliefs. In 2003 the company sold (for a 700% return on investment) its highly successful mortgage lending company, precisely for this reason. The $100 million price tag this divestiture brought can now be applied to fuel new growth, through new acquisitions and branches the company inaugurates as it expands to new markets.

Sterling has outperformed the market since well before its initial public offering in 1992, and has grown into a banking powerhouse with a Texas maverick's need to control its own destiny. Sterling realizes that the key to its continued independence (its goal is to be around for 200 years) is lasting outperformance. Towards that end, Sterling has staked out the ideal of becoming the "Perfect Company" defined by Sterling as simultaneous outperformance of stakeholder expectations in four critical categories: employees, customers, community, and investors. The company is a tireless local community leader for a variety of causes, including juvenile diabetes. And it has delighted investors with an average ROI

> A long-term view comes from some vision that gets declared, then living that declaration. In Sterling's case, that vision has been the desire to remain independent for 200 years.
>
> GEORGE MARTINEZ

for the last decade of over 16.5%. It exceeds its customer expectations continuously by deploying real, timely decision-making talent to the local front lines of Sterling's Supercommunity bank offices.

According to Richard Barrett, author of Liberating the Corporate Soul and creator of the related corporate sustainability assessment tool, Sterling Bancshares is the "Most Values Aligned" company that has emerged from studying hundreds of values-based companies.[19]

George Martinez suggests that living the company's core values as a "way of being" has created the context that has brought about the company's Superperformance and will carry Sterling forward through the next 200 years. When it comes to Sterling's shine, the company's signature slogan, "It's all about people, and always will be," says it all.

SYSCO: Food Distribution

Superfacts

- As of 2005 SYSCO is #1 in the industry based on profits, 10-Year EPS Growth, and 10-Year Total Return on Investment.

- Since the initial public offering in 1970, when sales were $115 million, SYSCO has grown to $29.3 billion in revenues for fiscal year 2004.

- SYSCO is the largest food distributor in North America.

- SYSCO eclipses the competition; it is larger than its ten next competitors combined.

- SYSCO is an acronym for Systems and Services Company.

Superstory

SYSCO was formed by John Baugh, a Houston food distributor, in 1969, after persuading the owners of eight other US wholesale companies to join him in founding a national food distribution company. Since then, SYSCO has grown into the largest food service distributor in North America. The company provides an inventory of over 275,000 products to more than 420,000 restaurants, schools, hotels, health care institutions, and other food service customers. SYSCO distributes fresh and frozen meat, poultry, seafood, fruits and vegetables, canned and dry products, paper and disposable products, cleaning supplies, kitchen equipment, and medical supplies. The company has a network of more than 160 facilities throughout the US and Canada.

Fiscal 2004 marked the 28th consecutive year of record sales and earnings for the company. SYSCO boasts economies of scale unparalleled in the highly fragmented food service industry. With $29 billion in annual sales, 420,000 customers, and the largest private fleet of trucks in the United States, the company is about equal in size to the total of its ten largest competitors.

This size allows SYSCO to support a nationwide distribution system, purchase products at the lowest prices from food manufacturers, and offer customers the widest selection of products. As the low-cost producer, the firm enjoys operating margins that are two to three times those of its competitors. SYSCO's private-label brands are the cornerstone of its competitive advantage. In fiscal 2004, they accounted for over 40% of SYSCO's $29 billion in sales.

> If you love what you do, you will never work another day in your life.
>
> CONFUCIUS

While it seems that honesty and truthfulness need to be mandated for some companies, SYSCO has been incorporating ethical dealing with employees, customers, and suppliers from its founding 35 years ago. SYSCO's ethics can be seen in the following company tenet: "The pound is to consist of no less than 16 ounces, and 100 cents of value must be exchanged for each dollar of revenue received." This commitment not only helps SYSCO's relationships with customers, it also forces the firm to measure virtually all its processes, an important part of SYSCO's success in a low-margin business.

SYSCO insiders enjoy the stature of the company; they proudly call it "the biggest and the best" in the food service industry. One insider applauds the company's flexibility in work schedules. Another associate asserts, "SYSCO makes a concerted effort to help employees achieve their career goals through comprehensive training."

While individual locations vary, dress code is typically "suit and tie when on the street." Fortunately, adds one insider, "there is a casual day the last Friday of every month. And the free food that makes its way around SYSCO certainly boosts office morale."

Over the last five years SYSCO has returned $2.7 billion, or 94% of its net earnings, to shareholders through dividends and share repurchases. Despite its size, SYSCO is poised to continue growing. With $29 billion in annual sales, SYSCO represents only 14% of the $200 billion food-service industry.

In SYSCO's 2003 Annual Report, in his Letter to Shareholders (commenting on SYSCO's spectacular performance), Richard Schnieders, SYSCO's CEO and Chairman, credited the people of SYSCO:

> Although we were extremely pleased with *what* occurred in FY 2003, the numbers tell very little about *how* SYSCO, during a very challenging time, continues to excel. In a word, it is the *spirit* of our associates, now more than 47,400 strong, as well as the entrepreneurial culture that fosters the autonomy of each and every one of our operating entities, that propels this company past all competitors. This Annual Report is dedicated to the women and men of SYSCO who have always found new ways, while operating within the strictest ethical guidelines, to help our customers succeed…. As we look to our future, it is bright, and it is bright not so much because of our market-leading technologies, although they are important. Our future is promising primarily because of SYSCO's people, and the human connections, from farmer to processor, from processor to SYSCO, from SYSCO to our customers, and from those foodservice professionals to their patrons. These relationships, imbued with dignity and respect, will sustain SYSCO and allow this great organization to continually provide a foundation for the foodservice industry.[20]

Tiffany & Company: Jewelry

Superfacts

- Tiffany & Young opened September 1837, inaugurating the non-negotiable sales price. The total sales for the day were $4.98.

- Tiffany's pioneered America's first store catalog in 1845.

- Tiffany's pioneered the 925/1000 American Sterling Silver standard in 1851.

- Tiffany and Young was renamed "Tiffany & Co." in 1853. In 1885 Tiffany's revised the Great Seal of the United States of America.

- In 1950, *Breakfast at Tiffany's*, by Truman Capote, was published, identifying the company's long-existing caché for a larger public.

- Tiffany's has an ironclad rule never to sell one of its trademark blue boxes; one can only be acquired for free with a Tiffany produced item purchased from Tiffany's, thus ensuring brand quality.

Superstory

Recognized the world over, the 161-year-old Tiffany & Co. brand stirs up images of design excellence, exquisite craftsmanship, and unparalleled customer service.

Tiffany & Co. was founded in 1837 by Charles Tiffany and John Young (originally named Tiffany and Young) as a retailer of stationery and costume jewelry. Soon the company introduced its trademark robins egg blue box tied with white satin ribbon (except during the Holiday season, when it changes to red). In 1845, the company started selling fine jewelry and published America's first mail order catalog. The company later expanded its merchandise offering to include silverware, timepieces, perfumes, and other luxury items. In 1853 Tiffany bought out his partners and renamed the business Tiffany & Co.

Over the years, the Company has built a solid brand, introducing a continuing stream of timeless signature design and luxury items, exclusively created by such world-renowned designers as Jean Schlumberger, Elsa Peretti, and Paloma Picasso.

In 1979 Avon Products purchased Tiffany's and then sold it again in 1984, when it was divested to a group of managers and private investors in a leveraged buy-out. In May 1987 the company went public and has been outperforming ever since, evolving to its current state of industry outperformance and a worldwide reputation for unparalleled excellence.

Today, Tiffany & Co. is a multi-channel retailer selling its proprietary jewelry, timepieces, sterling silver, china, crystal, and stationery through over 150 retail stores in 17 countries, its catalog, and the Internet, generating revenues of $2.2 billion in fiscal 2004.

I'm just crazy about Tiffany's.

AUDREY HEPBURN
BREAKFAST AT TIFFANY'S

What makes Tiffany's business model unique? Three things: First, the Tiffany & Co. brand is its greatest asset. The company has been around since 1837, and its name has become synonymous over the years with luxury, exquisite design, and fine jewelry. Tiffany's brand is as distinctive as its signature blue box. There is solid strength in the Tiffany & Co. brand—no doubt about it.

Second, Tiffany benefits from a strong international presence, which helps the company capitalize on the strength of its name. In 1972, it opened its first store in Japan, which has become its largest international market. Today, around 40% of Tiffany's total revenues come from international retail sales.

Third, Tiffany has literally raised its operating model to an art form, providing beautiful, superbly crafted luxury items and a distinct customer experience. Michael J. Kowalski, Chairman and CEO, has continued the company's strong commitment to outstanding quality, style, and customer service. With a continuous flow of new stores opening all over the world, the notably understated Kowalski has led the company through expansion of the product line, launch of the Tiffany web site, and recovery of the brand from wholesalers. The last change was made because the company believed it could better assure top quality and service if all aspects of Tiffany's business were kept in-house.

The company recognizes that its evergreen success depends on culture: the quality and dedication of Tiffany's people—its designers, gemologists, engravers, watchmakers, sales consultants, and other members of the Tiffany & Co. team. Encouraging personal growth and satisfaction, Tiffany trains and develops employees in the Tiffany experience. The culture is steeped in history and tradition, yet it reflects a contemporary personality, with an eye to the long view.

Toyota: Automobiles

Superfacts

- Toyota is a paragon of excellence. In 2005, for the fifth consecutive year, Toyota is the top-ranked corporation in the J.D. Power and Associates Initial Quality Study™, while its Lexus is the top nameplate for the fifth straight year.

- Toyota is Japan's largest company, employing 325,000 people all over the world in mid-2005.

- Toyota pioneered just-in-time (JIT) production methods and has applied continual improvement methods more rigorously than perhaps any other company in the world.

- Since it was instituted in 1951, Toyota's famous employee suggestion program has generated over 20 million suggestions.

- In an industry where upheaval is common, Toyota has not had a layoff in 50 years.

- Toyota began its life in 1926 as the Toyoda Automatic Loom Works. It began assembling automobiles in 1935.

Superstory

It is fascinating to watch so many companies try to imitate Toyota's Superperforming ways and miss the proverbial forest for the trees. Mainly they become mesmerized by the extraordinary Toyota Production System (TPS) and ignore (or misjudge) the role that culture, or what the company calls "The Toyota Way," has played in creating that system.

Onlookers are eager to acquire some of the magic that creates the top quality vehicles in the world, responsible for a continuous stream of outperforming sales and profits. They typically try to institute just-in-time (JIT) production, statistical process control (SPC), or continual improvement techniques. But they somehow miss the underlying element that breathes life into all of these tools. In their mechanistic pilgrimage for answers, the cultural dimension escapes them altogether. They do not see the complementary way these two hemispheres (process and culture) work together to form a complete whole—one that provides Toyota a tremendous competitive advantage despite the fact that its techniques and processes are well known.

> The Toyota way can be briefly summarized by the two pillars that support it: "Continuous Improvement" and "Respect for People."
>
> CARY CONVIS

In describing the interplay of process and culture, Gary Convis, President, Toyota North America says, "The Toyota Way, along with the Toyota Production System, make up Toyota's DNA. This DNA was born with the founders of our company and continues to be developed and nurtured in our current and future leaders."[21]

As with other Superperformers, Toyota's enormous success is derived from the marriage of process (efficient manufacturing operations, rigorous, disciplined, topnotch quality) and culture (the people that bring the process to life).

Toyota's story is legendary in the quality world. The company developed the vaunted Toyota Production System (TPS) that is the envy of manufacturers everywhere. The system has provided over a half century of continual improvement.

The Toyota system is a wonderful example of a Superperforming paradox: the extremely high quality that results from all of these manufacturing efficiencies also reduces costs. Years of consistently improving an already superior automobile has produced a premium brand for the company—a brand that entitles Toyota to a higher sticker price and remarkably steady profits in an unsteady industry.

Other automakers are not standing still. Quality and operating efficiency have been improving among US competitors, and new competitors have been entering the business from Korea and elsewhere. These may eventually present legitimate challenges. The industry dynamics could eventually catch up to Toyota. Still, the company keeps working to extend its lead.

Kaizen is the Japanese word for the philosophy of continual improvement that Toyota applies to everything. Hansei is the complementary Japanese word for continual reflection that Toyota insists is needed to create the true learning organization. Kaizen and Hansei work together to create Toyota's operating philosophy. While the pack is working feverishly to close the gap with Toyota, the "endless pursuit of perfection" it advertises in its Lexus slogan will continue to serve Toyota well.

Wal-Mart: Retailing

Superfacts

- In 2005 Wal-Mart topped the *Fortune* 500 list for the fourth year in a row.
- Wal-Mart is the world's largest employer with 1,500,000 employees in 2005.
- Wal-Mart's posted record 2004 earnings topped $10 billion for the first time.
- One out of every $7 spent on retail items in the world is spent at Wal-Mart.

- Wal-Mart's efficiencies are legendary. Studies by McKinsey showed that Wal-Mart alone contributed 12% of the nation's productivity increase from 1995 to 1999.

- Wal-Mart distributes just about any retail item anyone could need (from food to beauty products, together with clothes, electronics, domestic appliances, sports equipment, auto supplies, apparel, and more).

- In 1984, Sam Walton, Wal-Mart's legendary founder, danced the hula on Wall Street to pay off a bet with David Glass, then COO of Wal-Mart.

Superstory

For the last three years in a row *Fortune* has rated Wal-Mart one of America's top five admired companies. The company recently posted record 2004 earnings, continuing several decades of super-sized financial results. The title of Sam Walton's autobiography, *Made in America*, epitomizes what Wal-Mart represents to many: a real-life experience of the American dream. It is a story of abundant success arising out good old-fashioned American values: ingenuity, hard work, neighborliness, and thrift.

Yet, of all the Superperformers in the group, Wal-Mart faces the most significant hurdles. Its legendary founder Sam Walton instilled a set of principles described as full and complete partnership with employees and customers. The emergent culture of the early "Sam Walton Days" was a culture of teamwork: fun, challenge, and customer-mindedness. As Walton himself put it,

> Our relationship with the associates is a partnership in the truest sense. It's the only reason our company has been able to consistently outperform the competition—and even our own expectations.[22]

Today, Wal-Mart's multiple labor issues have been highly publicized, with Wal-Mart involved in several high-profile lawsuits. The company also faces the largest civil rights class action suit in history, as 1.6 million women charge the company with sexual discrimination in hiring, pay, and promotion.

In addition, the company faces significant legal and public-relations risks as the result of what some view as predatory labor and competitive practices. As it continues to expand, it is likely to face more pressure from unions and government agencies to change some of its ways. If the wind goes out of its cultural sails, Wal-Mart could slip from its vaunted Superperformance perch.

The company is the world's top retailer, with about 4,800 stores, including some 1,475 discount stores, 1,750 combination discount and grocery stores (Wal-Mart Supercenters in the US and ASDA in the UK), and 538 membership-only warehouse stores (Sam's Club). Nearly 75% of its stores are in the US, but Wal-Mart is expanding internationally; it is the number one retailer in Canada and Mexico. It owns 36% of Japanese supermarket chain SEIYU. Wal-Mart also has operations in South America, Asia, and Europe. Wal-Mart has become the world's largest retailer by coupling the lowest prices with the convenience of one-stop shopping for just about anything. Wal-Mart's Supercenter stores, which combine groceries with general merchandise, have been the company's fastest-growing division over the past five years.

> ## Dwell in Possibility.
>
> EMILY DICKINSON

Wal-Mart's ability to undersell its competitors stems in part from its low labor costs. Here Sam Walton himself was a champion for improvement:

> In the beginning I was so chintzy I really didn't pay my employees very well. The managers were fine....
>
> But we really didn't do much for the clerks except pay them an hourly wage, and I guess that wage was as little as we could get by with at the time. In fairness to myself, though, that was pretty much the way retail was in those days, especially in the independent variety store part of the business. It's just that in my early days in the business,

I was so doggoned competitive, and so determined to do well, that I was blinded to the most basic truth, really the principle that later became the foundation of Wal-Mart's success.....

The larger truth that I failed to see turned out to be another of those paradoxes....

And here it is; the more you share profits with your associates— whether it's in salaries or incentives or bonuses or stock discounts— the more profits will accrue to the company. Why? Because the way management treats the associates is exactly how the associates will then treat the customers. And if the associates treat the customers well, the customers will return again and again, and *that* is where the real profit in this business lies, not in trying to drag strangers into your stores for one-time purchases based on splashy sales or expensive advertising. Satisfied, loyal, repeat customers are at the heart of Wal-Mart's spectacular profit margins, and those customers are loyal to us because our associates treat them better than salespeople in other stores do. So in the whole Wal-Mart scheme of things, the most important contact ever made is between the associate in the store and the customer. I didn't catch on to that idea for quite a while.[23]

Today Wal-Mart's operating costs (mostly labor) are 17% of sales compared with 22% for Target. The firm faces multiple class action wage-related lawsuits, as well as a sexual-discrimination lawsuit in California that could become the largest in history. With 1.5 million employees (and plans for 2 million in five years), this Superperformer may be facing its largest challenge ever.

Summary

- Superperformers superperform over time.

- All Superperformers have developed super-adaptations that provide major advantages in their various industry niches.

- Superperformers yield extraordinary long-term profits. $25,000 invested in a hypothetical "Superperformance Fund" comprised of these ten companies twenty years ago would be worth $1.4 million today.

- Even in the short term Superperformance yields significant profits. That same $25,000 invested just ten years ago would yield a return of 420% today.

- The Superperformance Formula (PxC=SP) is exemplified in each of these Superperformers. In every case outstanding process combined with outstanding culture is the rule.

8 Simple Rules

RULE 1:   Process x Culture = Superperformance

RULE 2:   Superperformers superperform over time

RULE 3:   The paradigm shift of Superperformance is from Machine to Organism

Chapter 3

From Machine to Organism

Adopting a New Worldview

A s previously illustrated, Superperformance requires an entirely new worldview. Physicist Thomas Kuhn called this sort of fundamental change a *paradigm shift*. A paradigm shift trades one way of thinking for another. Paradigm means "framework of thought," from the Greek *paradeiknyai* (for "pattern"). To make a paradigm shift is to adopt a new pattern of thinking for understanding and explaining reality.

It is impossible to adopt a new way of thinking without letting go of an old one. In a paradigm shift, the change is a trade-out—an even exchange. And it is also discontinuous, not gradual. According to Kuhn, "Like the gestalt switch, it must occur all at once."[1] The

> Management theory and practice is shaped by a metaphorical process that influences virtually everything we do.
>
> GARETH MORGAN

new paradigm appears completely whole. Suddenly, the new reality is seen or recognized. Major advances always appear intuitively at first, as sudden revelations or flashes of illumination.

RULE 3: The Paradigm Shift of Superperformance Is from Machine to Organism

The operating paradigm for business for the past century has been Machine View. The new paradigm is Organism View.

Machine View

Machine View came into use in the eighteenth century as a product of the Industrial Revolution, and is the dominant paradigm still operating today. During the Industrial Revolution power-driven machinery became widely dispersed throughout the world. Machines were applied to agriculture, mining, and manufacturing, leading to the invention of the steam engine, steam ships, and railroads, and eventually to the industrialization of Europe and most of the western world.

We recognize the Industrial Revolution as the source of scientific and technological change in the world, but it was also responsible for a change

Organization as Machine   Organization as Organism

in thought itself. It popularized the view that the universe functions as a giant machine, exhibiting regular predictability, dictated by internal structure and function.

René Descartes (1596-1650), a French philosopher and mathematician, was the progenitor of this worldview. He proposed that the universe worked as a giant clock—with many interrelated but also separated parts.

Isaac Newton (1642-1727), an English astronomer and mathematician, built upon Descartes' ideas and developed out of them the fundamental principles we recognize today as modern mechanical physics. This Machine View of the universe provided the basis not only for the Industrial Revolution, the Scientific Revolution, and the post-Renaissance Age of Enlightenment, but it also gave birth to the view of organizations as machines. As one observer notes:

> During this period machines replaced agricultural workers by the thousands. The supply of unemployable armies of unskilled agricultural workers threatened the fabric of Western society. Then came a miracle, an ingenious notion of organizations. It was argued that in the same way a complicated tractor is built by parts, each performing only a simple task of horizontal, vertical, and circular motions, an organization could be created in such a manner that each person performed only a simple task.[2]

The essential feature of Machine View is that organizations are inanimate mechanisms with no intrinsic purpose. Organizations are simply tools whose attributes are defined by their operators to generate a profit.

The most important characteristic of the organizational machine is its dependability. Its structure is designed in. The parts have no inherent ability to reinvent themselves. A machine functions in a strictly linear cause-and-effect relationship between the parts.

Scientific Management

American industrial engineer Frederick Winslow Taylor (1856-1915), in his treatise *Scientific Management*, explained his theory of management by drawing on the same metaphor conceptualized by Descartes: the machine. In this way, Taylor translated the Machine View of reality into the archetype that still governs today's business paradigms.

Scientific Management became the panacea for industrial leaders in search of new organizing principles to deal with the emerging technologies, power sources, and labor-management relationships bursting forth at that time. *Scientific Management* gave birth to the first systematic approach to the management of organizations. It thus embedded the enduring metaphor of the machine deep into the organizational psyche of the western world.[3]

Machine View thinking holds that work can best be understood when we see the organizations we inhabit as mechanical devices to be engineered and rigorously controlled for clockwork efficiency. The endurance of

> ## The organization is an organism.
> PETER SENGE

this metaphor is nothing short of astonishing given the overwhelming evidence that it does nothing to address the intangible organization—the part that self-organizes, connects, engages, and *feels*.

Some old habits die *very* hard. Machine View, in its first generation, generated a production capacity for goods and services that surpassed the previous cumulative capacity for all of mankind! Not a bad paradigm for its time. Machine View was used in developing all the technology we take for granted in our daily lives today. There is much to applaud about Machine View. It was Newtonian physics, after all, that got us to the moon and back.

Even so, Machine View is incomplete. And when it comes to organizations, it is a major handicap.

Organizations are not machines; they are organisms. They grow. They emerge, self-organize, and co-evolve. Machines are capable of none of these behaviors. To mechanists business is strictly limited to the visible operations of the organization. Machine parts work essentially the same way from the moment they are placed into service until the moment they break down. They can be exchanged part for part, with no injury to the machine.

As Sterling Bancshares' George Martinez suggests, "The flawed idea is that every part of the system, including people, can be treated as *fungible* (even exchange, one for one, every part the same) with no economic or material damage to the system."[4]

This outdated worldview drives sub-optimization in many organizations today. A breathtaking number cling to Machine View, emphasizing short-term thinking, win-lose relationships, and strictly top-down, command and control methods.

These companies hold themselves prisoners to a paradigm dating back three hundred years! Its ideas come from an only half-right, reductionist paradigm of parts over wholes, tangible over intangible, visible over invisible.

Machine View has become increasingly detached from today's world of accelerating complexity, disaffected people, and the simple truth of Superperformance.

Organism View

Organizations are living organisms—biological and complex. When reexamined from this perspective, they make abundantly more sense. Along with all of nature, organizations share a certain polar-complementarity. In organizations, the two superpartners are process and culture. These twin forces are the catalytic converter, the core interaction at the fountainhead of organizational Superperformance.

ORGANISM	ORGANIZATION
Organelle	Sole Worker
Cell	Team
Tissue	Department
Organ	Division
Organ System	Group
Organism	Organization
Species	Industry
Ecosystem	Economy

Organisms and organizations contain natural hierarchical structures.[5]

The man who introduced Organism View remains remarkably uncelebrated, his wide-ranging, prophetic insights unappreciated or overlooked. In defending Organism View he rallied for a deeper scientific appreciation for organisms as whole, open systems, in stark contrast to the stubbornly mechanistic mindset of the physical sciences of his day.

His name is Ludwig Von Bertalanffy (1901–1972), father of General System Theory and champion of what he termed the "Organismic" view. Virtually all current improvement theory and practice has its roots in the systems thinking handed down by Bertalanffy—himself an early home-schooled biologist.

So it was from the study of life sciences that systems thinking emerged.

Regarding his early role in Organism View, it was said of him, "He was like Christopher Columbus. After him, it was not anymore necessary to discover America."[6]   He was nominated for a Nobel Prize in 1972 by twenty-first century icon of progress Buckminster Fuller, but died before the Oslo committee could consider his nomination. (Nobel Prizes are not awarded posthumously.)

To better characterize the continual process of change and stability (steady state) in open systems, Bertalanffy coined the German term *Fliessgleichgewich*, meaning "flowing balance." His work gave the world general systems theory, open systems, and process flow as fundamental elements of systems thinking.[7]

> The economy is not an engine, it's an ecosystem. And machines don't grow. Ecosystems do.
>
> STEVE GIBSON

It is exciting to discover in his original words a call for the expanded science that today so clearly explains the emergence of Superperformance. His thoughts (originally captured clear back in the 1940s) seem to peer directly into the future. He called for new science categories to explain the dynamic parts of living systems described best by self-organization, nonlinearity, and the like:

> If we look at a living organism, we observe an amazing order, organization, maintenance in continuous change, regulation.... However, concepts like organization, directiveness, teleology, just do not appear in the classic system of science. As a matter of fact, in the so-called mechanistic world view based on classical physics, they were considered as illusory or metaphysical. The appearance of models— conceptual and in some cases even material—representing some aspects of multivariate interaction, organization, self-maintenance, directiveness, etc., *implies introduction of new categories* in scientific thought and research.[8]

In these prophetic words, Bertlanffy put out an SOS for a new science to explain the parts of living systems that could not be described by ordered, predictable regularity. In his masterpiece, *General System Theory*, he further decries this missing explanation:

> It therefore appears that an expansion of science is required to deal with those aspects which are left out in physics and happen to concern the specific characteristics of biological, behavioral and social phenomena. This amounts to *new conceptual models* to be introduced.[9]

Bertalanffy recognized that organisms could not be completely explained by the classical science of thermodynamics available at the time, and saw a need for new ways to describe certain aspects of their behavior.

With the advantage of hindsight it seems obvious that Bertalanffy had seen the need for enlarging the life sciences to add the category we today label Complexity. Complexity theory, including the study of complex adaptive systems (CAS), the relatively new, rapidly advancing area of non-equilibrium physics, addresses the parts of nature that are nonlinear, self-organizing, and emergent. This extraordinary *new science* deals with the parts of life Betalanffy saw as outside the scope of both traditional biology and reductionist physics.

In one extraordinary leap of intuition, he provided with great clarity one of the earliest illustrations of "emergent" features at the whole, organism level:

60

The meaning of the somewhat mystical expression, "the whole is more than the sum of parts," is simply that constitutive characteristics are not explainable from the characteristics of isolated parts. The characteristics of the complex, therefore, appear as "new" or "emergent."[10]

In Search of a New Science

Bertalanffy's call was answered three decades later by Belgian chemist and physicist Ilya Prigogene (1917–2003). Prigogene used the mathematics of Complexity to identify *dissipative structures*, a new way to explain self-organization in living systems. He chose the term *dissipative structures* to emphasize the paradox of coexisting chaos and order reflected in self-organization. Prigogene was awarded the Nobel Prize in 1977 for a large body of work, including the discovery of dissipative structures. This ushered in the field of non-equilibrium thermodynamics and marked the birth of Complexity science.[11]

> Management is an organization's most important organ.
>
> PETER DRUCKER

In this way, Organism View is informed by a deep appreciation for the biology and physics at work in all living systems, including organizations. The new science of Superperformance is made of two sciences: biological science to inform the transformation of process, and complexity science to inform the liberation of culture.

The science of Superperformance is nothing less than a new management science. It is a life science, not a mechanistic science. It is based on 21st century scientific discoveries and replaces Taylorism, which is based on scientific discoveries dating back to the 16th century.

It is a call for nothing less than a revolutionary approach to how we think about business and organizations.

Summary

- The paradigm shift of Superperformance is from Machine to Organism.

- Machine View dates back to René Descartes' clockwork universe, and was the central metaphor of the Industrial Revolution. It led to the advent of Frederick Taylor's *Scientific Management*, the predominant management paradigm in practice today. Machine View holds that organizations can best be understood as machines, with interchangeable parts and reliable predictability, with no capacity to feel, create, or transform.

- Organism View, championed by biologist Ludwig Von Bertalanffy, recognizes that organizations are living, complex, adaptive organisms, with both linear and nonlinear dimensions.

- The new science of Superperformance is a life science. It is rooted in two polar-complementary sciences: improvement science to explain the transformation of process and Complexity science to explain the liberation of culture.

Section 2

The Properties of Superperformance

8 Simple Rules

RULE 4:   Superperformance is produced by super management and
          super leadership

Chapter 4

Leading and Managing Superperformance

Meet the Invisibles

U nleashing the *invisibles* is a powerful strategy for organizations in search of competitive advantage. The best of an organization's invisible assets—its intellectual and human capital—walks out the door everyday at 5:00 p.m.

These forms of capital are intangible. They are unrecognized on traditional balance sheets and have been historically under-appreciated— except by Superperformers.

For example, Toyota's remarkable just-in-time system and *Kaizen* philosophy are inextricably tied to the invisibles. They operate in a way that links optimization of the person and the system, generating over 50 improvement ideas a year per employee—over 96% of which are implemented.[1] Sterling Bank's amazing alignment of personal and organizational values is another powerful example, and has led to 1000 fold growth in 17 years, from $3 million to $3 billion in assets. Southwest Airlines and their egalitarian, zany culture in an otherwise buttoned- down business is still another example. Southwest enjoys a stunning market capitalization representing 70% of the entire airline industry's

65

value. For these companies unleashing the invisibles has led to a second-order performance in all areas.

There has never been a better time to leverage intangible assets. Organizations are struggling. Relentless complexity and operational urgency have become a way of life. Stress and Time Management have skyrocketed to the top of corporate training requests. In a recent report, Gallup found that over 70% of US workers are not engaged.[2] The best process in the world is DOA (dead on arrival) without the intrinsic energy and

> The value of a business increasingly lurks not in physical and financial assets that are on the balance sheet, but in intangibles.
>
> THE ECONOMIST, JUNE 12, 1999

desire to implement it. Until now, the power of these hidden assets has been hugely undervalued (and untapped) by most organizations.

Approaching Breakpoint

Capturing and optimizing these capital assets requires a new set of skills. As management theorist Peter Drucker asserts, in this new age, knowledge workers have the leverage, and they carry their means of production along with them wherever they go. According to Drucker, "The critical feature of a knowledge workforce is that knowledge workers are not 'labor,' they are capital. Knowledge based businesses need to be... focused on the productivity of their capital."[3]

As a result, leadership and management are on the verge of a major transition. While Drucker insists that management is the organization's most important "organ," he also argues it is not possible to "do it" to people. Rather, he declares, "the task is to lead."[4]

Lloyd Provost and the other Deming masters at the consulting group Associates in Process Improvement (API) teach us that it is only processes that can be managed, and only then through the purposeful application of continuous testing and learning (using the scientific method).[5]

Business futurist Esther Dyson draws on the new science of complexity to characterize this impending transformation through a different lens. In her view, idealized leadership and management must act as a sort of organizational "immunity," capable of manifesting and acting wherever and whenever needed.[6]

Leaders and Managers are the Same People

Understanding how Superperformance happens calls for a fresh inquiry into the properties of leadership and management. This introspection yields a monumental discovery: there is an inherent chaos and order to leading and managing Superperformance.

RULE 4: Superperformance is Produced by Super Management and Super Leadership

---

Superperforming leadership and management are actually best appreciated as *polar-complements*! They are two sides of one coin. Super-leading has to do with vision, influence, and inspiration—use of gifts that *energize culture*. Super-managing has to do with order, predictability and control of systems—use of gifts that *orchestrate process*. One amplifies the culture, the other operates the process.

These two hemispheres work together to create a company that is everything it can be. A cadre of great leaders who can inspire impassioned devotion to the cause but who cannot conduct a process will not survive for long. Likewise a brilliantly engineered operating plan that ignores the influence and involvement of the people who will implement it will inevitably fail. High marks in *both* areas are required to produce lasting success. Superperformers have simply discovered and applied this fundamental truth.

Super Management	...with...	Super Leadership
Orchestrates Process		Energizes Culture
Involves System Factors		Involves Human Factors
Focuses Head Down		Focuses Head Up
Is Anchored in Reality		Looks Toward Possibility
Standardizes		Creates
Integrates		Self-Asserts
Asks How and When		Asks Why and What
Controls Work		Liberates Passion

Leadership and Management Everywhere

Companies that live in Machine World operate in a steady state of underperformance. They are hardwired with narrow definitions of leadership and management that squander intellectual capital and smother intrinsic motivation. In Machine World leading and managing are considered the exclusive domain of the people at the top of organizations. In today's dynamic and complex business environment, this approach is incomplete and dangerous.

Superperformers have evolved beyond Taylorism, recognizing that today's business world is so unpredictable, competitive, and risky, that survival depends on mobilizing every ounce of energy and intelligence. Machine World definitions cannot sustain a company in this new environment.

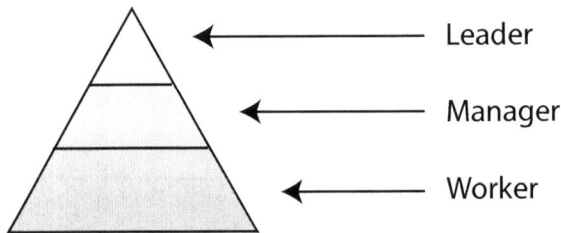

The traditional organization.

Superperformers know that even the very best efforts of the small group of people at the top are insufficient to provide any lasting advantage. Instead of constraining the use of these mission-critical capabilities to top executives, these organizations transmit management and leadership *everywhere*. They equip people at every level with the knowledge, skills, and power to act meaningfully, just-in-time, and just-in-context, on behalf of the organization. In this world leadership and management are distributed properties, in the same way the nervous system is a *distributed property* of the body and intelligence is a distributed property of the brain. Here *everyone* is called to lead and manage. Here leader/managers transform process and liberate culture at every level. In this way, Superperformers *radiate* leadership and management everywhere.

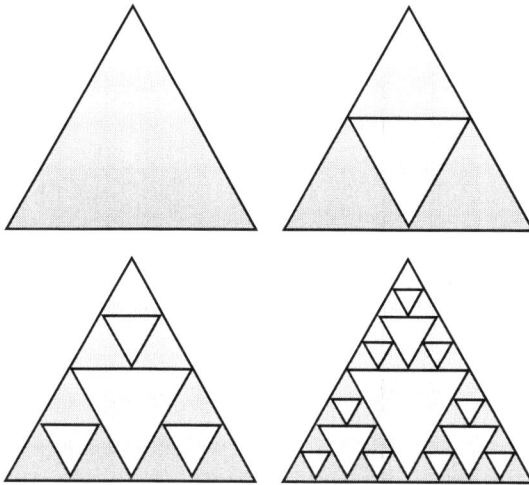

Superperformance distributed fractal: Everyone a Leader/Manager.

Advantages to a Distributed Leadership and Management Approach

- Involves everyone.
- Reduces any sense of entitlement.
- Unlocks the full capacity of the organization.
- Releases the hero inside the organization and inside every individual.

- Distributes and greatly expands the leadership (of people).
- Distributes and greatly expands the management (of process).
- Releases "managers" from bondage of "managing people."
- Shifts to system of work as primary organization chart.
- Institutes leadership and management as a way of being.
- Simplifies operations.
- Spreads organizational DNA to every member.
- Allows ownership and control (of process) to come from both the top down and bottom up.
- Encourages growth of the individual.
- Encourages joy in work.
- Increases self-esteem of the individual.
- Increases individual responsibility.
- Increases "felt" ownership by the individual.

Introducing the Ten Habits of Leader/Managers

The key to lasting success at anything has to do with habits. A habit, from Latin *habere* (to have), is a pattern of behavior, practice, or custom acquired through frequent repetition. Good or bad, most of our daily activities are habitual. Father of Psychology William James has said that habits are "stronger than ten natures."[7] This means there is a *tenfold* greater power in a habit than in ungoverned human nature. In a surprisingly short time, habits form furrows in our unconscious minds and become instinctive and automatic. For example, we drive a car through the power of habit. What would it be like to have to *think* through synchronizing use of the turn signal, steering wheel, brake, and rearview mirror every time we made a turn? Most of what we do, and how we do it, is controlled by unconscious habit. What does habit have to do with Superperformance? Everything.

Superperforming leader/managers can be distinguished by their habits.

Following are ten Superperforming habits that can be acquired by anyone and strengthened like muscles with repeated use. By adopting these, anyone can increase personal mastery. They are divided between five habits of leadership and five habits of management. They can be applied at any scale to amplify process and culture. They are explored further in the next two chapters.

Habits of Management	Habits of Leadership
Focus	Inspiration
Continual Improvement	Empowerment
Simplicity	Empathy
Project Management	Creativity
Systems and Statistical Thinking	Integrity

Formal Structures and Superperformance

Leading and managing Superperformance is not a call to revoke formal authority and chain of command. All Superperformers maintain formal structures. Formal structures define process ownership, reporting relationships, and span of control. This chain of authority is an unbroken line of reporting relationships that extends throughout the entire organization to provide governance, direction, accountability, and security. Superperformers have formal decision-making structures that help people know who they are accountable to, and where to go with a problem. Superperformers don't abandon or devalue the formal system; they know it is requisite.

> It will not suffice to learn all about the present style of management. One could learn everything there is to know about ice, but know nothing about water.
>
> W. EDWARDS DEMING

What distinguishes Superperformers is the complementary presence of a robust *informal system* to balance the formal system, a network of *nonlinear relationships* to balance the linear reporting system, and a *bottom-up energy* to complement top-down execution. Superperformers know intuitively there is a fundamental need for both.

In the future, all workers will need to know how to improve a process, work in a team, test a theory, or implement a change. These traditional capabilities will be even more essential in a more rigorous Superperforming landscape. But workers will also need to acquire new skills, such as enrolling others, using small-scale testing, nourishing intrinsic motivation, and dealing with surprise.

Fitness Landscapes: Co-Evolving in an Ever-Accelerating World

Organizations do not operate in static worlds. To survive, they must co-evolve with their environments. Stuart Kauffman, evolutionary biologist and complexity pioneer, has proposed that all living systems inhabit "fitness landscapes," and that each searches for a point of optimum fitness in that environment.[8]

In the same way, Superperformers are constantly improving themselves by searching out new peaks of fitness, or new places of competitive advantage in their own "fitness landscapes." They are on an unending pilgrimage to find better ways to achieve results. But landscapes evolve and are constantly changing. Organizations have to co-evolve to

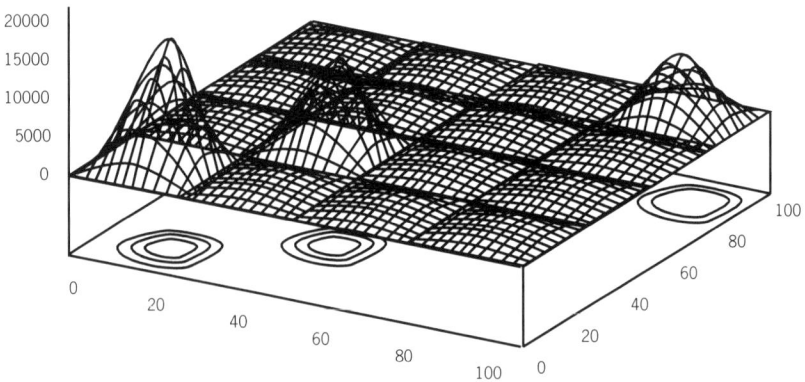

Organisms inhabit Fitness Landscapes.

stay in tune and maintain fitness. The challenge is to shift back and forth between the hemispheres as needed.

For example, the typical pattern is to follow the start-up stage of a new business with a process standardization stage. This is a job for Management, rather than Leadership. Management keeps organizations operating in a predictable way.

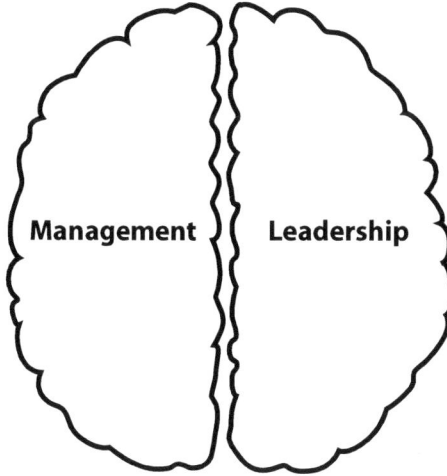

Leadership and Management are Polar-Complements.

But environments constantly change. There are always new customer needs, competitive behaviors, societal twists and turns, technological changes, and so on. But Management, by definition, has a "head down" orientation. Organizations with that orientation may fail to notice important changes quickly enough. Over time, an organization can become less and less in sync with its environment, increasing dissonance. What they need at this point is the "head up" orientation of Leadership.

Leaders would question: "What is really going on here?" "How do we regain relevance?" "How do we fulfill our purpose given these new circumstances?" Leadership seeks to bring organizations more in line with the changing environments they inhabit, which often requires changing the very processes they have worked so hard to stabilize. And yet, as Leadership engages people in these questions, it can summon new purpose and energy.

Superperformance requires constantly switching back and forth between management and leadership. The oscillation creates an emergent identity radiated by the entire organization. From Sterling Bancshare's empowered community of *bankers*, to the extraordinary gentility of the Tiffany and Co. consultants, to the road rallies Harley-Davidson field reps conduct for its worldwide Harley Owners Group (HOG), every employee of a Superperforming organization sends out a powerful beam of light that references the company's *super* identity.

Lead People, Manage Process

Lead people, manage process. The task of Superperformance can be summed up in this simple proverb. It means that the *polar-complementarity* of process and culture is the same *polar-complementarity* of leadership and management. It also means, especially in the area of complexity science, that there is a great deal of new knowledge to acquire and apply. Making the most of the visibles and invisibles

> Lead people, manage process.
>
> SUPERPERFORMANCE PROVERB

together requires a new paradigm and new actions. Improvement and complexity science provide the necessary tools.

As today's organizations look for better business practices, leading people and managing process re-focuses attention from building the machine to growing the organism. Superperformance is a call for gardeners, not mechanics.

Once organizations embrace Superperformance principles, they will discover profoundly more effective—and surprisingly simple—new strategies for action.

Summary

- Unleashing the *invisibles* is a new trim tab for organizations in search of competitive advantage. The power of the invisibles—human and intellectual capital—are woefully under-appreciated by most organizations.

- Because of this new awareness, the practice of organizational leadership and management are on the verge of a major transition.

- Superperforming leadership and management are *polar-complements*, two sides of one coin: Leading has to do with vision, influence, engagement, and inspiration (use of gifts that *energize culture*), while Managing has to do with order, predictability and control of systems (use of gifts that orchestrate *process*). Leadership and management must work together to create an organization that is everything it can be.

- Superperformers see leadership and management as *distributed properties*—they transmit these capabilities to everyone.

- There are Ten Habits of Superperforming Leadership and Management. These will be explored further in the next two chapters.

- Formal leadership and management structures are vital parts of Superperforming organizations. But by balancing these with informal structures, Superperformers greatly increase felt ownership, action taking, and creativity in the organization.

- The work of Super Leaders/Managers can be summed up in this simple proverb: "Lead people, manage process."

8 Simple Rules

Chapter 5
Transforming Flow

Reframing Deming

Statistician W. Edwards Deming is generally considered the father of modern quality science. Deming used and expanded upon methods (such as the PDSA [Plan-Do-Study-Act] Cycle and the Control Chart) acquired from Walter Shewhart at Western Electric in the 1930s. Deming is credited with supplying the knowledge that informed the miraculous transformation of post-WWII Japanese manufacturing, leading to Japan's tremendous economic growth throughout most of the last half-century. Deming's theories were *rediscovered* in the US in the frenetic quality movement of the 1980s, and are generally regarded as fundamental tenets of contemporary quality practice.[1]

Deming outlined his "System of Profound Knowledge" in his last book, *The New Economics*.[2] It presented four integrated components in a comprehensive theory for optimization of an organizational system:

Appreciation for a System

Organizations are systems comprised of interdependent parts with one common aim. Management's role is to strive toward optimization of the system as a whole.

Knowledge of Variation

Variation is always present. An understanding of variation leads to informed decisions to reduce it. Using an understanding of variation to inform decisions is the antithesis of the prevailing practice of "reacting to the last number."

Theory of Knowledge

Management's job is prediction. Prediction is based on knowledge, and knowledge is built on theory. "Experience without theory teaches nothing."[3]

Knowledge of Psychology

Knowledge of individual and group psychology is needed to nurture and preserve the interactions of people, to preserve and nurture their intrinsic motivation, creativity, and joy in work.

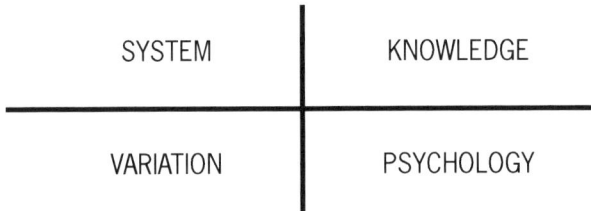

SYSTEM	KNOWLEDGE
VARIATION	PSYCHOLOGY

These four components are usually presented together in a way that suggests they should be equally weighted. In truth, most quality consultants and companies themselves focus on the "concrete" aspects of Deming philosophy, working diligently to institute systems thinking, improvement, and statistical control methods.

But is this the best interpretation of Deming's System of Profound Knowledge?

These four elements are described as interdependent, but in fact, the fourth component, Psychology, undergirds and energizes the other three. Psychology, from the Greek *psyche* (for "soul" or "spirit") is the part of transformation having to do with people.

In describing this element Deming himself wrote:

> Psychology helps us to understand people, interaction between people and circumstances, interaction between customer and supplier, interaction between teacher and pupil, interaction between a manager and his people and any system of management.[4]

Regarding optimization of business and other social systems, Deming held passionately that nothing short of revolution was called for. He titled his last book "The New Economics" to underscore the need for "metamorphosis" in education, government, and business. He wrote:

> We are living in prison, under tyranny of the prevailing style of management, interaction between people, between teams, between divisions. We need to throw overboard our theories and practices of the present, and build afresh.[5]

The Superperformance formula (PxC=SP) reframes Deming to capture the fundamental importance of Psychology in the transformation of a system. This new view of Deming emphasizes the *polar-complementarity* of technical and human factors.

SYSTEM	/	VARIATION	/	KNOWLEDGE

PSYCHOLOGY

In this way the Superperformance formula recasts Deming's Profound Knowledge Model into two equally-weighted hemispheres.

This is more than just a novel reconstruction. Countless organizations have adopted Deming's teachings yet somehow underestimated or ignored

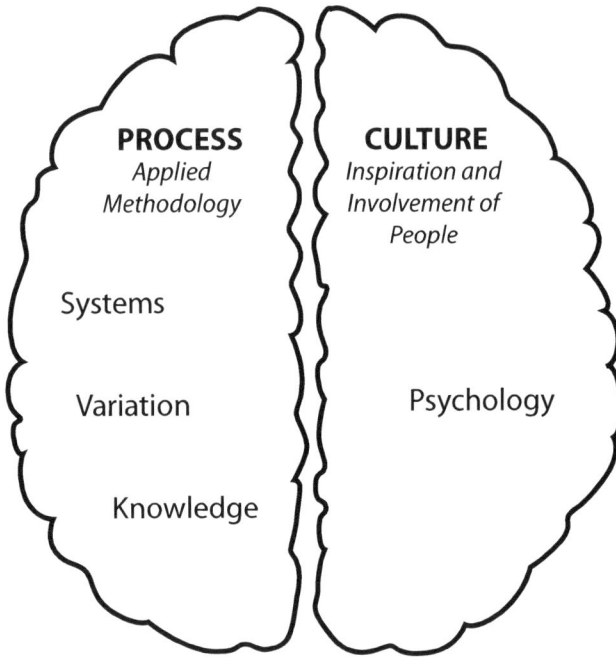

PROCESS
Applied Methodology

CULTURE
Inspiration and Involvement of People

Systems

Variation   Psychology

Knowledge

New Profound Knowedge.

the fundamental requirement for involved, motivated people. Many Total Quality Management (TQM) programs undertaken since the 1980s have failed to achieve anything more than a few sparks of flash performance and have seen performance slip back to pre-engagement levels, or worse. Only those organizations that have elevated the inspiration and involvement of people to the same level of importance as process mechanics have achieved any sustainable improvement of quality, service, costs, or profitability.

Transforming Flow

Transforming flow is Job 1 on the process side of Superperformance. Flow is the internal process stream in an organization, a requisite property of all living systems. Organizations are the same as any other organism when it comes to this property. The better the flow, the healthier the organism.

Here are some examples of process flow:

System Type	Flow Type
Human	Blood-flow
Community	Information-flow
Organization	Work-flow
Economy	Money-flow

If it were possible to take an X-ray of an organization, its physiology would mirror its flow of process, comprising the organizational "system of work."[6] This view is also called the organizational *production system* (for example, the Toyota Production System; Toyota uses the concept of "one-piece flow" to visualize the organization as one flowing stream of production).

RULE 5: Superperformance is Transformed Flow

Processes flow in a continuous loop through customer-supplier relationships, from inputs to throughputs to outputs, and back around, driven by the feedback of customers and the environment.

In healthy organisms, flow occurs at every level. It can be found at the aggregate system level as well as at the most fundamental operating level. A guiding proverb that applies at every scale is, "The next process is the customer."

These same concepts and principles apply to other living systems, providing a basis for some general themes. Organizations are organisms. They contain properties found in other organisms: open system, system-environment boundary, inputs, outputs, throughput, feedback, steady state, hierarchy, aim (teleology), interdependence of parts, and co-evolution. All of these biological properties can be found in organizations.

Biological Patterns

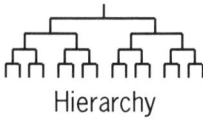

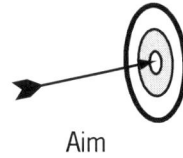

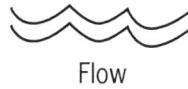

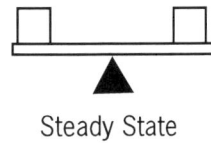

Hierarchy

Aim

Flow

Feedback

Steady State

Optimize the System vs. the Parts

Why focus on optimizing the whole system instead of the individual parts? System theorist Russ Ackoff shows that a strategy of optimizing the individual components (making every part the best it can be) will sub-optimize the system. Everyone doing his or her best will *not* create the best system.

> The performance of the whole is not the addition of the performance of the parts, but it is a consequence of the relationship between the performance of the parts. It is how performance relates, not how it occurs independently of the other parts. That is what systems thinking is about.[7]

Optimization of parts fails to recognize that the properties of the whole, at the system level, are emergent and different from properties found at lower levels. Biologists often cite a classic riddle to illustrate this principle:

Question: What do you get when you dissect a cat (to examine its parts)?

Answer: A dead cat.

Machine View seeks understanding by reducing everything to its constituent parts. Organism View, on the contrary, seeks understanding (of the organization) at the whole system level, *where performance relates*, bringing an organization's emergent global identity into focus.

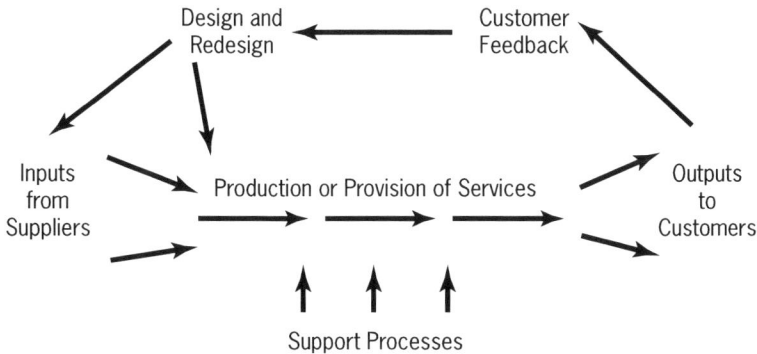

Deming's Production Viewed as a System.[8]

Common Limitations

Most of contemporary improvement practice is limited in two ways: (1) programmatic approaches and (2) preoccupation with technical over human transformation factors. Superperformers enable and accelerate transformation by addressing both of these conceptual flaws. While internal performance consultants are the focus of the most educational depth and intensity, Superperformers reach all areas of the organization to learn, make changes, and improve at a far more rapid pace than is normally possible.

While individual project savings are often possible, some of the most important improvements have to do with long-term "top line" issues: the reduction of organizational complexity, and improvements that delight customers. Superperformers bring to reality Deming's call to action in his 14 Points: "Put everybody to work on the transformation."[9] Led by informed practice and development initiatives, success can be replicated at a pace rarely seen, even in large organizations.

How do Superperformers Transform Flow?

What are the process habits of Superperformers? What is the technical arsenal that these companies use to transform flow? Superperformers eschew programmatic approaches and initiatives. Yet Superperformers are consistent, highly reliable performers. They resist bureaucracy and waste. Instead they are robustly engaged in the use of a few simple habits. These habits generate consistently groundbreaking performances in every Superperforming case. From Sterling Bank's split-second information transfer to the local desktop of front line managers, to Southwest Airlines' astonishing 15 minute arrival-to-departure time, to Toyota's miraculous 15 month concept-to-automobile prototyping time, there is something second-order going on in every one of these core processes. Transformed flow dramatically changes an organization. What are the methods Superperformers use to transform flow? A full review of these tools is beyond the scope of this book and unnecessary in view of the extensive literature in the field, but a fundamental overview is required.

> The living systems view allows us to see organizations as dynamic, rather than static systems.
>
> LLOYD PROVOST

Transformed process flow arises from the rigorous practice of certain habits. These are distinguishable from the level of practice found in sub-performing organizations. A critical distinction is that in Superperformers, these represent common enterprise habits, not just habits restricted for use by formal management or even project teams. These management habits are distributed to every employee. On the process side these include focus, continual improvement, simplicity, project management, and the conscientious use of systems and statistical thinking.

The Habit of Focus

Ingraining Constancy of Purpose

Persistence is a survival trait of every successful organism. Superperformers are no exception. They stay on target and are relentless in their pursuit of their second-order performance goals. They instill constancy of purpose and are able to focus it like a laser on their strategic initiatives.

> # A goal without a method is nonsense.
>
> W. Edwards Deming

Without constancy of purpose organizations face an uphill battle. They will become easily distracted by new directions, short-term thinking, and unnecessarily wasted energy. Superperformers are superb at focusing, relentlessly perfecting their mainstay process, which through countless iterations is typically refined to an unparalleled degree.

The Habit of Continual Improvement

Applying Kaizen: Always better

For organizations, fitness improvement is process improvement. Process improvement is driven by new knowledge gained and applied throughout the system. Second-order change (the kind of improvement that occurs by fundamentally changing the system) is mostly an achieved state, arising from successive learning cycles of process improvement created over time.

API's Model for Improvement is a wonderful example of a process improvement model designed to optimize fitness. The Model for Improvement is an extraordinary tool because it is perfectly suited for the paradoxical requirements of going fast and sure. Its beauty is that it doesn't require a huge output of study before change can commence. Rather, it advocates small-scale tests of change and learning, documented in successive cycles of experience.

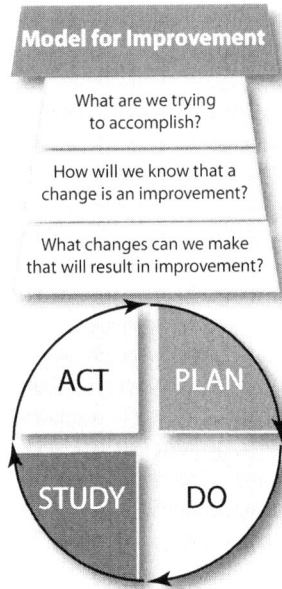

The Model for Improvement.[10]

Adopted successfully by large and small organizations in many industries, the Model for Improvement is appealing because it greatly simplifies the improvement process. It asks three questions and includes the essential PDSA cycle. That's it. Anyone can understand and apply the Model. Its simplicity is the key to its powerful scalability.

OTHER TOOLS USED FOR CONTINUAL IMPROVEMENT

Besides the requirement for a robust improvement method, there is a basic arsenal of tools that facilitate continual improvement. Four to six of these can handle most (80%+) of the heavy lifting of improvement—these can be widely dispersed and template driven.

Some of the primary tools, in typical order of use are:
- Purpose Statement.
- Improvement Team Charter.
- Process Flow Diagram.
- Pareto, Histogram, Control Chart.
- Process Knowledge, Knowledge for Improvement.

- Knowledge of Variation.
- Cause and Effect Diagram.

The Habit of Simplicity

Eliminating Waste in All Forms

Superperformers keep it simple. They resist bureaucracy. They eliminate rework. They avoid new policies and procedures when a simple guideline will do. They remove unnecessary steps. This mentality leads to eliminating waste in all forms.

In short, Superperformers operate lean. The aim of lean is simple: removal of unnecessary complexity. To operate lean is to relentlessly eliminate waste in every area of operations. Because every part of the organization touches, depends upon, and supports the mainstay process in some way, Superperformers insist on enterprise-wide involvement in lean.

> The less effort, the faster and more powerful you will be.
>
> BRUCE LEE

The theory of lean operations was first introduced after World War I in Japan. Elji Toyoda and Taiichi Ohno of the Toyota Motor Company pioneered the concept of lean production. This concept was popularized in the early 1980s by a book called *The Machine that Changed the World.*[11] Lean production, in short, is "lean" because it aims to use less of everything. This means less human effort, less floor space, less resources, and less time to develop a new product or services. Taken together, these advantages lead to a greater and ever increasing variety of products and services. Simplicity is the ultimate goal of lean operations. By eliminating waste in all of its many forms, simplicity is what remains.

The Habit of Project Management

Applying Project Management Methods

Self-management is keeping promises, managing finances, meeting deadlines, planning work, setting goals, and monitoring progress. These processes, when translated to the larger organization, are the elements of project management.

Superperformers know that project management provides many advantages—including bottom line impact. Project management is the application of knowledge, skills, tools, and techniques to a broad range of activities in order to meet the requirements of a particular project.

Learning without action is not learning.

PROVERB

According to the Project Management Institute (PMI), project management is comprised of five processes—Initiating, Planning, Executing, Controlling, and Closing—as well as nine knowledge areas. These nine areas include Project Integration, Project Scope, Project Time, Project Cost, Project Quality, Project Human Resources, Project Communications, Project Risk Management, and Project Procurement.[12]

Project management helps Superperformers meet their customers' needs by standardizing routine tasks and reducing the number of tasks that could potentially be forgotten. Superperformers use project management to ensure that available resources are used in the most effective and efficient manner. Project management provides insight into "what is happening" and "where things are going" within organizations.

Project management helps Superperformers to:
- Organize large-scale efforts.
- Incorporate leadership and management.
- Enable customer focus and alignment.
- Quantify value.
- Optimize the use of organizational resources.
- Put strategic plans into practice.
- Ensure faster time-to-market.

The Habit of Pattern-Seeking: Systems and Statistical Thinking

Thinking Systemically

Superperformers are systems thinkers. They know that in order for an organization to transform flow it must first understand itself as a system. For many organizations, this requires a new vocabulary and a new set of ideas. Many systems thinking concepts can be counterintuitive, even opposite of what people have learned in the past. But without this new knowledge, organizations cannot become all that they can be.

Systems are comprised of interdependent parts with one common aim. "Without an aim there would be no system."[13] For example, if all of an individual's body parts suddenly decided to launch out in different directions, there would soon be no "individual." In an organization, optimization comes when the aim of the organization is understood and shared by everyone in the system, and all the parts cooperate to accomplish the system's aim. Understanding a system in this way makes it easy to see why cooperation is the highest form of self-interest—and the only way to get an organization to operate at its peak.

Thinking Statistically

Superperformers are statistical thinkers. This means they use an understanding of variation to guide decisions. Where is variation found?

Variation is everywhere. No two things in nature are exactly alike. People are different. Arrival time for an airplane or a train varies. Most variation can be seen with the naked eye, but some variation is so slight it can only be detected with sensitive instruments. Some common examples of daily variation are personal finances, behavior, or weight over time.

The key to reducing variation lies not only in measuring it, but also in understanding what is causing it. Variation comes from many sources. Although some variation in system performance is due to differences between workers, most is not. The largest percentage of variation is built into the system of work itself.

Although the causes of variation are many, the use of statistical methods can help us to understand and manage it effectively. In particular, the goal is to know whether the variation observed is the result of: (1) something special going on, or (2) simply random occurrence.

To live in falsehood is worse than death.

ZEND-AVESTA

The cost of misinterpreting variation can be high. Superperformers use an understanding of variation to look for the inherent patterns in data instead of responding exclusively to individual events.

Knowing the type of variation present in a process leads to different actions to manage it. This also helps to avoid two common errors that are frequently made in interpreting data: (1) tampering (treating a stable system as if it were unstable) and (2) under-controlling (treating an unstable system as if it were stable).

Future Simple

There is extraordinary power in applied simplicity. Simple methods can be scaled for tremendous gain. Focus, continual improvement, simplicity, project management and systems and statistical thinking offer a powerful arsenal for transforming flow. Together these habits form a robust set of modern improvement theories and technical methods.

Summary

- The Superperformance formula (PxC=SP) recasts Deming's Profound Knowledge Model into two equally weighted hemispheres. This new view of Deming emphasizes the partnership of technical and human factors.

- An organism's fitness is inextricably linked to its ability to adapt and improve itself, which is governed by its ability to measure and improve its process flow. This requires the continual improvement of the system.

- A paradox of systems thinking is that a strategy of optimizing the individual elements (everyone doing their best) over a strategy of optimizing the system leads to sub-optimization. When individual parts become the focus for improvement, the system will be shortchanged.

- Systems are structured hierarchically. They consist of different levels of process. According to the mechanistic view, a lower level view is all you need. If you know the precise performance of each department or team, you should be able to understand how the organization functions. Organism View, instead, argues that such a paradigm misses the most important thing: the organization is a whole organism.

- The five process habits are (1) focus, (2) continual improvement, (3) simplicity, (4) project management, and (5) systems and statistical thinking. These habits work interdependently to amplify the process dimension of Superperformance.

- Superperformers gain extraordinary power through applied simplicity. The right knowledge scaled can provide tremendous amplitude.

91

8 Simple Rules

RULE 1:   Process x Culture = Superperformance

RULE 2:   Superperformers superperform over time

RULE 3:   The paradigm shift of Superperformance is from Machine to Organism

RULE 4:   Superperformance is produced by super management and super leadership

RULE 5:   Superperformance is transformed flow

RULE 6:   Superperformance is unleashed passion

Chapter 6

Unleashing Passion

A Felt Cause

Organizations are in highest integrity, from the Latin *integer* (for "wholeness") when they are inspired with the fire of a felt cause. Whether that cause is to create the best software on the planet, design the world's finest jewelry, or supply humankind's healthcare product needs, Superperformers are passionate about what they do.

At Harley Davidson, for example, leaders came to realize they needed a revolutionary cultural change. Echoing Deming, Richard Teerlink championed a radical new approach to leadership:

> Leaders can no longer look at themselves as being the fountain of all wisdom, the world's best problem solvers, or the only ones who are responsible for its results. People as clients and employees are a company's only sustainable competitive advantage! When leaders understand this, the next step is to take responsibility for the operating environment that people walk into every day. It's important to differentiate your products and processes in some characteristics. But our differentiation really was based in employee commitment. We believed that if employees identify with the company and its purpose they help create the appropriate competitive advantage.[1]

93

Superperformers fill their different industry niches with miraculous form and function. From airline to automobile, they are the most important companies in their fields, setting the standard and capturing the lion's share of market capitalization for entire industries. And they know that their passion is their most valuable intangible asset.

RULE 6: Superperformance is Unleashed Passion

Living in Revolution

Organizations experiencing the continuous emergence of Superperformance operate in a sort of living revolution. There is no mistaking the thrill of it. Like surfing, life is most exciting out at the front of the wave, where it is breaking. Superperformers not only operate at this edge, they own it, and *moreover*, are able to remain there indefinitely, continually emerging anew.

This level of energy can only be sustained with the highest sense of purpose. This kind of resolve doesn't wither with challenge but only grows stronger, more resolute, more certain. This kind of commitment comes from doing it for *love*.

> We all have reservoirs of life to draw upon, of which we do not dream.
>
> WILLIAM JAMES

Superperformers are powered by people who love their organizations and whose organizations love them back. They are inspired revolutionaries who are intrinsically—not extrinsically— motivated to do what they do. As Berkshire Hathaway's Warren Buffett describes this felt arrangement, they are employees inspired to "act like owners."[2] These people are highly committed because they are operating in alignment with personal values and purpose. This continuous emergence illustrates the principle of the *rich get richer*, or increasing returns.[3] The principle holds that you tend to get more of what you've been getting. Success tends to snowball, in the same way a snowball traveling downhill gets larger by gathering more snow around itself. Eventually, it becomes so large that it triggers an avalanche. In this case, what is produced is an avalanche of outperformance: return on investment, return on equity, return on assets—over time, return on just about everything.

Superperformers truly, genuinely care about their people. This deep regard for the spirit of the organization is nuclear in Superperforming companies. It comes from deeply rooted company values and ideology. Every individual matters. Every job counts, regardless of its position on the organization chart. Gain sharing is a fundamental, universal feature. An atmosphere of dignity and respect prevails. These companies have created a level of optimism, encouragement and respect for the individual that brings out the *Superhero* in people, provoking a level of commitment that soars far beyond what ordinary companies can muster.

> My ideas have undergone a process of emergence by emergency. When they are needed badly enough, they are accepted.
>
> BUCKMINSTER FULLER

In Superperforming companies, community is a much larger fusion than what can be created by conventional teambuilding. Superperformers know that everyone in the organization is organically connected and that nonlinear relationships strengthen the system, as with any family.

Superperforming communication is active, interactive, and cross organizational, not just top-down, constrained to functional silos or even to multifunctional teams. Openness is a behaved value, not just a formal declaration of intent. Diversity is abundant and new ideas are explored and implemented faithfully. The result is that everyone knows what the company's priorities are and feels a *personal* sense of ownership for the company and its success. In this way, the organization is able to function as one super team.

The Trivial Many

The vast majority of organizations, by comparison, operate with underdeveloped right brains. This disability creates fundamentally flawed, often dehumanizing, and sometimes even bizarre behavior. This affliction guarantees under-performance and can easily lead to crippling internal competition, anxiety, and fear. The current slew of literature addressing the worst disasters in this Sahara of lost potential describes it all as so much "toxic waste."[4]

> The uninitiated are those who believe in nothing except what they can grasp in their hands, and who deny the existence of all that is invisible.
>
> SOCRATES

Rarely does this occur because of corrupt corporate leaders. In fact, the root cause of this disease is ignorance. The truth of Superperformance has simply not reached the boardroom of most companies. Governed by mechanists, they continue to operate with the conviction that the visible part of the organization is the only part that matters. The result has been to perpetuate the "idiot-savant" model of organization man: technically brilliant but empathically challenged. This hapless Frankenstein of Machine View has been the dominant theme in business management since the Industrial Revolution.

The price of this disability has been considerable: untapped intrinsic motivation, squandered intangible assets, and needless under-performance.

Turning Point: Seeds of Revolution

The growing awareness that sustainable outperformance is governed by simple rules, the relentless rise in business complexity, and the alarming increase in the emotional detachment of workers—all signal an approaching shift, a turning point.

We are on the cusp of a new era in business. Culture matters...*hugely*. And it can no longer be ignored.

More and more companies recognize they are sub-optimized in Machine View. As obsolete management practices give way, a new fitness landscape will emerge, led by Superperformers in many different areas. As more and more companies see the simple truth in the Superperformance formula (PxC=SP), they will work to revolutionize corporate culture— to create one that unleashes frustrated

> # Revolutions never go backwards.
> ANONYMOUS

Superheroes, liberates dormant organizational right-brains, and sets average companies on the path to becoming *wonderful* companies.

Surely some companies will disappear. As Deming cautioned, "Survival is optional." Nature shows us that as with any evolutionary change, some learn and adapt while others resist and eventually die out. Some companies will achieve the higher peaks of the new fitness landscape, while others will sink into a deep valley where the old ways simply do not work anymore.

Complexity Patterns

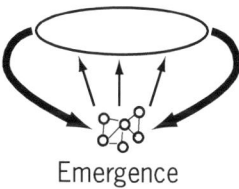

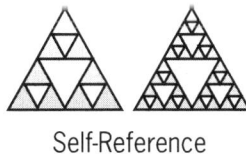

Emergence

Increasing Returns

Self-Organization

Edge of Chaos

Self-Reference

A New Science for Culture

Superperformers know that people on fire with a felt cause create *fantastically* better products and services. They use this understanding to leverage the full potential of the organization-employee partnership. While to Superperformers this truth is intuitive, there is an emerging new science that informs this phenomenon, revealed through the complex adaptive patterns of organizations. Using the new lens of complexity, we can finally examine the intangible parts of organizations and recognize self-organization, attraction, nonlinear interactions, self-reference, increasing returns, and emergence at the edge of chaos. Complexity science provides the night-vision goggles to illuminate the invisible world of culture.

Growing Evidence that Culture Matters in the Literature

The Superperformance Formula (PxC=SP) works because process and culture are polar-complements. Interestingly, the organizational performance literature has been validating the essential culture hemisphere for quite some time. This is evident in a number of classic studies, including Jim Collins' *Good to Great* and *Built to Last*, Tom Peters' *In Search of Excellence* and *Passion for Excellence*, Jeffrey Pfifer's *The Hidden Factor*, John Kotter's *Culture and Performance*, and so on.

In Search of Excellence	Built to Last	Good to Great	Warren Buffett	Fortune 500 CEOs
People	Stretch Goals	Passion	Long-term Appeal	Management
Management	**People**	Great Idea that	Broad Appeal	Team
Team	Management	Works	**People**	**People**
Purpose	Team	**People Win**	**Practices**	Action Oriented
Action Oriented	Action Oriented	Execution	Large Cap	Highly Regarded
Creative	Innovative	Discipline	Innovation-Minded	by Experts
Company with a	Highly Regarded	Level 5 Leaders	Super Form/Lean	Close to
Past	by Experts		Management	Customer
Close to			Great Business	Innovation
Customer				Performance
Financial				
Performance				

Importance of People Appears in Every Study.

The variable of "people," in one way or another, appears as a critical success factor on every list. No other single variable is common to every study of organizational excellence—the remaining variables representing a variety of mostly technical factors.[5]

How do Superperformers Unleash Passion?

Superperformance requires passionate people. But passion emerges; it cannot be imposed. The new science of complexity confirms this hidden principle. Understanding how passion emerges leads to a powerful revelation: there is an unsung Superhero trapped inside everyone.

The idea that there are different types of corporate culture is a myth. When it comes to performance, there is only one continuum: outperformance on one end and underperformance on the other. All organizations fall somewhere on the continuum. Regardless of organizational personality, style, or core process, this principle holds true.

Superperformers are diverse. But they all use a common set of habits to revolutionize culture. These include the habits of inspiration, empowerment, empathy, creativity, and integrity.

The Habit of Inspiration

Engaging Everyone in a Felt Cause

Superperformers capture the hearts and minds of their people. Inspired people bring a powerful energy to any cause they believe in. They are emotionally connected to the company and its goals.

These people have entered into a *covenantal* relationship with the company. A covenant has much deeper meaning than a contract. A covenant is a deeply felt partnership based on trust, while a contract is a temporary partnership based on distrust. In Superperforming organizations, people trust the company to reciprocate their commitment. They are intrinsically motivated to help make the company all it can be.

This kind of commitment cannot be purchased and cannot be imposed; it must be willfully volunteered.

The Habit of Empowerment

Awakening Desire and Unleashing Superheroes

Superperformers let their people run. They know there is greatness in them, so they encourage and expect them to achieve more. They ask them to take ownership and make decisions. They equip them with the capabilities they need, and they help them to grow. They remove obstacles and reward initiative. They push authority to the lowest possible level, so that everyone can make use of their unique talents and gifts.

Leaders who empower are preoccupied with enlarging the cultural environment. They instinctively appreciate the power of encouragement and recognize there is huge unrealized potential in people and organizations. Leaders who empower know that their principal work is to foster the growth of others.

A favorite story illustrating the power of empowerment is the story of Seabiscuit, the legendary racehorse. Seabiscuit did not fit the classic definition of a champion. He was a scrawny, undersized horse with knees that wouldn't straighten, a foreleg that jabbed sideways when he galloped, and a mean, erratic disposition. He floundered at the bottom rungs of horseracing for years, until he was

> Every man for himself is a recipe for disaster.
>
> ERNEST SHACKLETON

acquired in 1936 at a rock bottom price by Charles Howard, former bicycle repairman and automobile entrepreneur. Over the next four years Seabiscuit would shatter over a dozen track records, culminating in a world-famous contest with Triple Crown winner War Admiral, in a spectacular match that is *still* regarded as the greatest horse race in history.[6] What was the magic formula that unleashed the hero in Seabiscuit?

In a word, freedom. Tom Smith, Seabiscuit's laconic trainer, came to realize that, through mismanagement and maltreatment, Seabiscuit's full potential had never before been appreciated. He knew instinctively that the solution was to "let him run." Like Seabiscuit, every individual and every organization has a Superhero trapped inside. This Superhero emerges *for free* in response to encouragement, trust, and freedom to run.

> Your purpose is to discover your work, and then with all your heart, to give yourself to it.
>
> <small>BUDDIST PROVERB</small>

Freedom to run does not mean freedom to run *wild*. Empowerment is always given with boundaries. Boundaries are required so that changes in one part will not adversely affect other parts of the system, so that the larger system purpose will be served, and the system will operate effectively.

Empowerment should not be confused with entitlement. Empowerment without responsibility is entitlement. Entitlement squanders the potential of the organization and wastes resources. A sense of personal responsibility is pervasive in Superperforming companies. Responsibility coupled with empowerment will produce amazing results.

The Habit of Empathy

Fostering Emotionally Intelligent Interactions

Superperformers relate to people. They tune in to people's needs. They pay attention to their wants, and they honor their feelings. Because they fundamentally value people, they recognize the power of community and work to strengthen informal relationships and bonds.

In a classic *Harvard Business Review* article, Daniel Goleman, Emotional Intelligence guru insisted, "IQ and technical skills are important, but emotional intelligence is the *sine qua non* of leadership."[7] Goleman defines emotional intelligence as mastery in five areas:

- Self-Awareness—the ability to recognize and understand one's own moods, emotions, and drives, as well as their effect on others.

101

- Self-Regulation—the ability to control or redirect disruptive impulses and moods. The ability to suspend judgment, think before acting.
- Motivation—the propensity to pursue goals with energy and persistence. A passion to work for reasons that go beyond money or status.
- Empathy—the ability to understand the emotional makeup of others. Skillful dealing with people according to their emotional reactions.
- Social Skill—proficiency in managing relationships and building networks.[8]

A touch of empathy can transform sterile interactions into stellar relational events, electrifying employee and customer relationships. The growth of community may not have been the anticipated outcome, even so it is a powerful benefit that arises when people cooperate to achieve a shared vision. Superperformers know you can't get to the best outcomes without passing through the door of relationships.

The Habit of Creativity

Being Open to Novelty and Change

Superperformers are almost universally their industry's foremost innovators. Novelty is in their blood. They use creativity in everything—from problem solving to process design, from strategy to service, from corporate law to corporate learning.

How do Superperformers keep ideas flowing? They know that just telling people to be creative won't do it. They do much more than that.

For example, Toyota's famous employee suggestion system generates an average of 51 ideas per employee per year, 96% of which are implemented. This is a tremendous influence in a company of 325,000 employees. How does Toyota sustain this extraordinary level of creativity?

Toyota has:

- Leaders that honor and encourages ideas from everyone in the company.
- A system structure for implementing ideas (including a secretarial staff for helping to track and support the implementation of ideas as well as provide the syndication of suggestions across the company.
- Front-line supervisors who are as pivotal in promoting suggestions as they are critical in translating these suggestions into real changes.[9]

Superperformers create the right environmental conditions for creativity to happen, and they follow through to turn ideas into action. By cultivating an environment of openness, experimentation and learning, they make the company a greenhouse for new ideas.

> ## To advance from the ordinary requires a new game, or a new territory.
>
> KEVIN KELLY

Most importantly, they make it safe to fail. They know it is important to try out many new things to make the connections that will lead to the real breakthroughs. Superperformers know that the only companies who never make mistakes are the ones who never try anything new.

Today, the business case for innovation is implicit. As change and choice accelerate, more and more companies are looking for creativity and innovation to save the day. Those companies who celebrate openness, learning, and experimentation will find the breakthroughs they need.

The Habit of Integrity

Instilling Evergreen Values and Insisting on Transparent Behaviour

Berkshire Hathaway's Warren Buffett is notoriously scrupulous on the importance of integrity. After taking the helm of Salomon Brothers in a bond trading scandal in 1991, he famously warned Salomon's managers,

"Lose dollars for the firm and I will be understanding; Lose a shred of reputation for the firm and I will be ruthless."[10]

Johnson & Johnson did not equivocate when faced with the Tylenol crisis. In 1982, seven people in the Chicago area died after taking Tylenol™, a popular pain-killer manufactured by McNeil Consumer Healthcare, a division of Johnson & Johnson. The Tylenol they ingested had been laced with cyanide, and for weeks it wasn't clear whether the capsules had been tampered with during the manufacturing process or after leaving the factory.

Johnson & Johnson immediately recalled some 31 million bottles of Tylenol, worth approximately $100 million, sent 500,000 letters outlining the situation to physicians, hospitals and Tylenol distributors, and set up a toll-free hotline for consumers. All of this Johnson & Johnson did for the simple reason that it was the "right" thing to do. The company's long-standing credo, which puts the well-being of customers first, was the compass Johnson & Johnson credited for solving the Tylenol crisis.[11] Johnson & Johnson's response to the Tylenol scare is one of the most inspiring and referenced examples of corporate responsibility in history.

> Integrity is more important than technique.
>
> MIKE MARKKULA

Superperformers hold themselves to a higher standard. They are trustworthy, honest, and ethical. They regard their corporate reputations as a sacred trust. They live by an inviolable set of principles and do not compromise them. In this world of ethically challenged organizations, this is a refreshing rarity. Superperformers value transparency in all of their reporting and communication systems, and their stakeholders credit them with a higher valuation for it.

Process and Culture Together: A Lasting Marriage

Before Superperformance, we have seen initiatives for improving process or culture come and go as independent fads management becomes excited by—until the next one comes along. Now that new learning from biology and complexity science has finally reached the business world, we can see that process and culture are interdependent parts of living, complex adaptive systems. This family of management and leadership habits must become a permanent way of life for organizations to become everything they can be.

Summary

- Superperformers are powered by the energy of a felt cause.

- Superperformers operate with the awareness that the passion they engender is their most valuable intangible asset.

- Most organizations operate with a dormant, underdeveloped right brain. This gives rise to a disabling "idiot-savant" image of organization man: technically brilliant but empathically challenged.

- Superperformers use five habits to revolutionize culture and move to the outperforming end of the spectrum: inspiration, empowerment, empathy, creativity, and integrity.

- This family of management and leadership habits must become a permanent way of life for organizations to become everything they can be.

The Transformation to Superperformance

8 Simple Rules

Chapter 7

Upshifting to Superperformance

Transformation to a New Steady State

Upshifting to Superperformance requires a system transformation to a new steady state. This transition is similar to the change that occurs when water turns to ice.

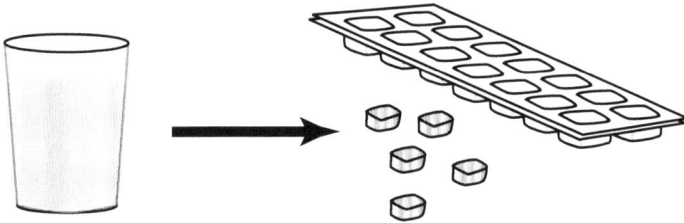

Transformational changes of this type abound throughout nature: the epidemic transmission of a virus, the critical mass of a runaway social trend, metamorphosis of a caterpillar into a butterfly, and even certain emotional changes, like the process of falling in love. The change is comprehensive and dramatic. Scientists call this a *phase transition*, a state change that occurs without altering a system's underlying chemical composition.[1] Phase transitions are sudden, non-linear, and system-altering.

The physics of a phase transition are analogous to transformational change in other systems, including organizations. In a phase transition, as the energy, temperature, or information passing through the system increases, the threshold is approached and crossed, provoking a sudden system-level change.

First the system is operating at one level, then suddenly, another. At this critical threshold, at the tipping point, the system reaches a high level of disequilibrium, then finally gives way, becoming fundamentally altered and restablized in a new steady state.

RULE 7: Superperformance Requires Metamorphosis

To upshift to Superperformance is to undergo this same fundamental change. This is a change to a different way of being, a new organization. To echo Deming, what is required for transformation is not "mere patchwork on the current system," but "metamorphosis," a change so fundamental that something new is created.[2]

Metamorphosis and transformation both come from the same Greek root, *metamorphoo* (meaning "to transform" or "to get a new form"). To achieve Superperformance is to morph into something unprecedented, something new, as from a caterpillar into a butterfly.

When a caterpillar crosses from the larval stage into the chrysalis stage on the way to becoming a butterfly, it enters a period of metamorphosis. What happens during this stage?

The Chrysalis Stage: The Pattern Revealed

The chrysalis stage is one of nature's wonders. Enzymes are released that digest the caterpillar tissue, converting it into a rich culture medium. Contained inside the tissue are several sets of dormant cells in different parts of the body. As the metamorphosis begins and as the chrysalis forms, these tiny cells undergo a revolutionary growth spurt. The chrysalis provides a culture medium for these cells to grow. These cells specialize into new body parts: the wings, organs, legs, antennae (all new), as well

> "How does one become a butterfly?" she asked pensively. "You must want to fly so much that you are willing to give up being a caterpillar."
>
> TRINA PAULUS

as muscles, the entire digestive system, heart and nervous system, which existed in the caterpillar before and are now completely recreated.[3]

Like the dissipative structures discovered by Prigogene in Chapter 3, the process is self-organizing, paradoxically bringing alive new structures while dissipating old ones.

According to Deming, nothing short of metamorphosis can create an organization that is everything it can be. As the caterpillar is re-created to become a butterfly, organizations must be re-created to become Superperformers.

Phase transitions are always associated with an increase in energy, information, or temperature. During the development of the adult butterfly, the chrysalis loses nearly half of its weight.[4] This shows that the experience of metamorphosis consumes tremendous energy. In the same way, upshifting to Superperformance, which involves instituting new habits and surrendering old ones, will consume tremendous energy.

Statistically speaking, this is called a second-order change. Statisticians make a clear distinction between first- and second-order changes to a system. First-order change will only maintain the current state. But a shift to Superperformance requires a second-order change, a fundamental change to an altogether new state, a new system.

First-order change:
- focuses on maintaining the status quo.
- brings processes back into statistical control.
- adjusts the current system.
- involves doing more or less of something.
- is non-transformational.

While second-order change:
- involves a fundamental system change.
- is a shift to a new steady state.
- requires new learning.
- is a transformation to something new.

Environmental Forces in Superperformance

In any organization, there are environmental forces that either support or limit transformational change. Understanding and addressing these forces is important. Examining them throughout the Superperformance journey helps people in the organization know what they're up against.

For most organizations, the single biggest impediment is the status quo. ("We're already successful, so why change?") But when transformational change becomes a pressing survival issue, companies are in a better position to take on the challenge and achieve Superperformance. They will change—because they have little choice.

Companies that have enjoyed moderate to average success over time may not feel a pressing need to change. They are the ones least likely to create something lasting.

Coming to believe in the real possibility of achieving the transcendent results of a Superperformer can be a daunting psychological barrier. It seems easier to bandage the current system, or simply continue fighting fires and doing business as usual. Organizations facing this challenge should explore the inestimable cost of not changing.

Following are two lists of transformation drivers and barriers:

TRANSFORMATION DRIVERS

- A collective understanding of why Superperformance is necessary.
- Comprehensive learning about Superperformance.
- A clear desire for Superperformance.
- Distributed management and leadership.
- A spirit of shared ownership for the transformation.
- Persistent willfulness to engage and implement change.
- Time (patience).
- Allocation of resources.
- A plan to acquire new habits and surrender old habits.
- Acknowledgement of the fear associated with change.
- Prepared responses for expected resistance.
- A balanced system of metrics for process and culture.
- A focus on customers.
- Awareness of the influence of sub-cultures.
- Tangible rewards for everyone engaged in the transformation.
- Links between all transformation efforts and long-term vision and purpose.

TRANSFORMATION BARRIERS

- Ignorance of Superperformance.
- Fear of failure.
- Machine View leadership and management.
- Empowerment without responsibility.
- Responsibility without empowerment.
- Short-term thinking.
- Change driven only from the top.
- Change desired only by the bottom.
- Change without involvement or discussion of people affected.
- A canned transformation program.
- Pressure for instant results.
- Impatience with learning.
- Appropriate resources unavailable.

- Comfort with the status quo.
- Reward systems that affirm win-lose.

The Kryptonite of Superperformance

In the move to achieve Superperformance, organizations should avoid practices that weaken process and culture and sap their strength. We call these practices the Kryptonite of Superperformance.

1. Performance Appraisal and Forced Ranking

Performance appraisal and its attendant companion, forced ranking, do nothing to improve a system. In fact, these outdated practices obliterate collaboration and cooperation, serving only to trap people in artificially constructed boxes. These practices diminish joy in work and create a competitive environment of "every man for himself." People are pushed to compete, to be perceived as better than their co-workers. They are rewarded for carefully guarding information, instead of sharing it, and taking credit to themselves, instead of giving it away.

> Money often costs too much.
>
> RALPH WALDO EMERSON

A survey by the Society for Human Resources Management found that more than 90% of performance appraisal systems are unsuccessful.[5] One reason performance appraisal fails is because it is not scientifically possible to objectively evaluate people. More importantly, people need to be encouraged, not discouraged. People interpret mediocre ratings as a lack of appreciation. Realizing this, managers are reluctant to conduct appraisals, often procrastinating for months.

This interaction, which could be a wonderful opportunity to encourage and enroll people in the company's cause, actually does the opposite. Performance appraisal destroys intrinsic motivation, and can, in the space of twenty minutes, transform vibrant, highly motivated and committed *associates* into deflated, resentful *hirelings* sapped of company loyalty and self-esteem. The overwhelming majority of people on both sides of the table dislike the process. Performance appraisal actually obstructs, instead of encourages, genuine feedback.

Yet many organizations, caught in the snare of Machine View, continue to conduct them.

Everyone needs feedback. But feedback is much more likely to be heard and accepted when people seek it out for themselves. Optimal feedback should be totally separated from pay and promotion.

SUPER REMEDY:

Stop performance appraisal and forced ranking. Instead focus everyone's collective energy on achieving the company's goals. Give people the freedom to seek out and receive feedback, with the goal being to improve the company. Redesign feedback, coaching, compensation and promotion processes to encourage and motivate people to win together.

2. Short-Term Thinking

Wall Street's obsession with current earnings has produced a generation of attention-deficit business executives. Financial scandals and suspect accounting are the most obvious symptoms. Far more insidious is the corrosive effect that short-term thinking has had on organizational decision-making. Focusing on current earnings to the exclusion of everything else ironically forces managers to ignore their primary responsibility—protecting and increasing company value.

Most of this destructive behavior is related to misplaced incentives. Wall Street rewards executives and their companies for reporting incessantly increased earnings. One lapse and Wall Street transmits a "sell" signal. The company's stock price then declines, shareholder confidence wanes, executive careers (tied to performance) become imperiled, and then there's a panicked scramble for "instant pudding."

This bizarre system begets bizarre behavior. The dozens of major firms named in a variety of recent scandals have all responded to this pressure by artificially manipulating finances. Fabricated revenues, disguised expenses, off-balance sheet partnerships and hidden liabilities colluded to inflate profits. Creative accounting assured the unbroken advance of higher and higher quarterly earnings. For a while, investors were ecstatic. But for many companies, like Enron, WorldCom, Adelphia and others, the chickens of flash performance finally came home to roost.

Superperformers operate with a time horizon of forever, refusing to fall sway to short-term thinking. As Sterling Bancshares George Martinez explains, "A long-term context affects every decision and every interaction."[6] Sub-performers, in contrast, are driven by expedience. Anything that interferes with the next quarter's earnings—people, quality, research and development, safety, maintenance, workforce development—must be ruthlessly sacrificed. Otherwise the CEO will lose his job. Short-term thinking is

> ## No man is free who cannot command himself.
> PYTHAGORAS

expensive and damaging. It creates endless upstream and downstream repercussions, wastes resources, and drives needless complexity. Its strategies are designed to find a quick fix for a current problem, relieve some pressure, or merely create a false impression of improved performance faster. It affirms mediocrity, destroys quality, and in the extreme leads to ethical lapses and flawed decision making.

SUPER REMEDY:

> Stop short-term thinking. In its place institute and reward long-term thinking. Incorporate an understanding of variation.

3. Wrong CEO

The Chief Executives of the ten Superperformers profiled in this book all came from inside their companies, reflecting an average tenure of 29.4 years. (The number two executives in these ten companies followed a similar pattern of longevity.) This is in dramatic contrast to an average tenure of just 6.2 years for the CEOs of the number two companies in these industries (several recently installed by their boards in response to a crisis). Simply put, Superperforming top executives are long-term company people who understand and deeply care about their organizations.

Sub-performers, on the other hand, favor the new breed of "Flash CEOs" ready to take the helm of any company at a moments notice to put things right. These new hired guns are usually charismatic, quick on the draw (the quicker the better) and capable of making things happen *now* in a withering assault.

CEO Years With Company

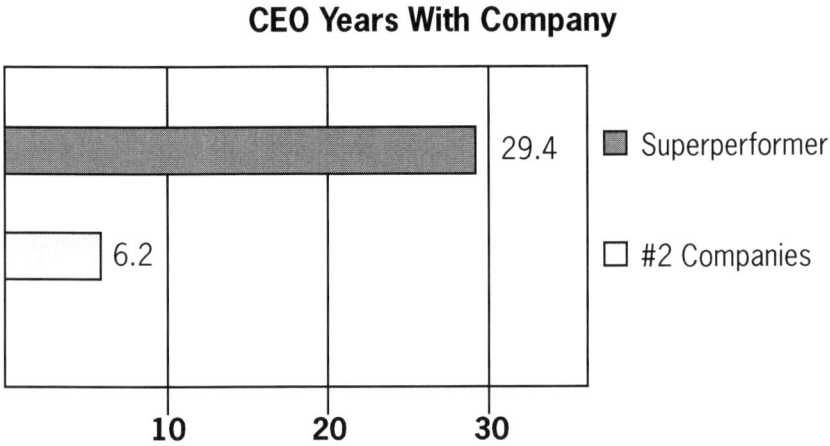

There is something basic about the way these CEOs relate to their companies that makes them different from previous generations of corporate managers. Several decades ago Richard Barnet and Ronald Müller predicted in their book *Global Reach* that the new breed of "monetary executives and marketing experts" would have "little personal interest or direct pride in their products" and would be unlikely to show a "passion for quality or technical excellence."[7]

A short-term executive that is not going to remain in a company for more than 5 years does not have the same (economic or emotional) stake in the company of a 20-, 30- or even 40-year executive. They won't fret much if the reputation or quality of the company disintegrates after they leave. All that matters is today's current earnings. The popular business literature extols their greatest virtue as the capacity to execute. The theme is "CEOs fail because of bad execution."[8] As simple as that—not getting things done, being indecisive, not delivering on commitments quickly enough. Alacrity above all.

Flash CEOs are a dangerous product of short-term thinking.

Hence, the job of CEO is increasingly difficult to hold onto these days. In contrast to Superperforming CEOs, the average tenure of CEOs in large corporations is shrinking, today averaging well under a decade.[9] The desire for "instant pudding" has become the relentless focus of Wall Street and Main Street alike. In an effort to demonstrate the ability to execute, clearly talented leaders are led to make rash decisions, alienate valuable people, miss important opportunities, and sacrifice just about everything to "make the numbers" for the next quarterly earnings report.

> We cannot become what we need to be by remaining what we are.
>
> MAX DEPREE

In a very short period, the wrong CEO can destroy a company. The business landscape is littered with companies who have lost their focus at the whims of the wrong CEO. Companies will turn prodigious energy toward making even the most hare-brained ideas of top corporate leaders seem positively ingenious, falling into the all-to-familiar trap Warren Buffett terms the "institutional imperative."[10]

SUPER REMEDY:

Install a CEO with an appreciation for Superperformance and a passion for the company, its people, and its products. Search first for a long term company executive.

4. Weak Ethics

Numerous accounting scandals have rocked the business world

recently, causing stock prices to tumble, resulting in lost investor confidence. This has led to the famous Sarbanes-Oxley legislation, prompting onerous new levels of financial accountability, transparency and disclosure.[11]

Like the wrong CEO, weak ethics can destroy or severely damage a company in a very short period. Fortune 500 companies, scores of mutual fund managers, and countless individuals have been damaged because of weak ethics. Typically, greed at the top (and sometimes throughout) is the root culprit. While outright criminal fraud is cited in only a small percentage of cases, the challenge of weak ethics is more of an endemic corporate problem than a specific company problem.

In many of the culpable companies, a surprising number of people knew and went along with the deceptions and irregularities. How could this happen?

Deming often used the parable of the "frog boiling in water" as a metaphor for imperceptible gradual decline. If you place a frog in boiling water, he will try to escape. If you place him in cold water and heat it gradually, the frog will remain in place until he's boiled to death, because gradual change is not perceivable.

The lesson is that an investor culture that continues to reward greed and short-term performance over long-term organic value will continue to produce greedy, ethically-challenged individuals who continue to deliver flash performance. As the Law of the Harvest declares, "You reap what you sow."

Superperformers strive to maintain a "way of being" that is uncompromisingly ethical. While no Superperformer is perfect, all of these companies enjoy deeply rooted and rigorous ethical standards. Superperformers use various means to maintain these standards. They include:

- *Corporate Values*—The principles the company considers important about the way they do business.

- *A Code of Conduct*—A written code of conduct that everyone is expected honor, available for reference at all times.

- *Ethics Committee*—Typically, a standing committee of the board of directors that provides oversight to the company ethics program.

- *Ethics Education*—Education in how to deal with potential ethical situations.

- *Ethics Communication Channels*—An "ethics hotline" as recourse for employees who have a personal ethical issue to deal with, or who wish to make an accusation of wrongdoing.

- *Continual Evaluation*—A continual improvement process for evaluating the effectiveness of the company's ethics programs, incorporating recommendations from all levels of employees.

SUPER REMEDY:

Implement ethical standards, insisting on board-level accountability. Enroll everyone continually. In the case of ethical lapses at the top, root out the culpable individuals and install new top management. Determine what cultural influences led to the breakdown and address them to prevent a recurrence.

5. Mergers

The ten Superperformers profiled in chapter 2 have all made a variety of acquisitions. These have been typically small, undertaken for strategic reasons or because the target company was vertically integral to the company's core business. But none have ever merged.

It is common knowledge that mergers misfire at a disturbing rate; over 75% failing to deliver anticipated returns.[12] Predicted synergies rarely reach a level that justifies the premium paid at acquisition.

Why is this? One reason may be that in addition to all the technical factors (financial, market, legal) attention is rarely paid to the culture of the target company. Merging companies tend to limit due diligence to how financials line up, and neglect intangible aspects.

Given the negative history of mergers, what in the world would drive a company to pursue such a risky strategy?

Advocates claim, above all, that mergers will increase shareholder value. Executive officers may have a few hidden motives as well:

> There are very few inferior people in the world—only inferior environments.
>
> FRANK LLOYD WRIGHT

- *Desire for a Quick Fix*—Often mergers are pursued because the company is under pressure to produce instant results. But, as we know, short-term strategies usually produce long-term problems.

- *Potential Compensation of Executives*—Often, merger terms are set up to benefit specific executives orchestrating the deal; they will receive stock options and other performance related payments.

- *Potential Compensation of Deal Makers*—Lawyers and investment bankers initiate and enthusiastically promote mergers. They receive compensation based on the size of the deal.

- *Ego*—The potential to emerge as a much larger or conglomerated company can be seductive. But will the merged company truly strengthen and support the acquiring company's core purpose and identity?

SUPER REMEDY:

Don't merge. Instead, acquire carefully, with a particular eye to core purpose, values, and cultural alignment. If you do merge, concentrate on creating one single purpose, one system of work, and one company identity, all focused on Superperformance.

6. Learning Disability

Superperformers are learning organizations. They exhibit "maximally changeable" form and function while holding firm to unchangeable purpose and values. In contrast, sub-performing organizations cling stubbornly to old ways, refusing to consider or embrace new knowledge. These are organizations with a learning disability.

Companies with a learning disability grossly underestimate the dynamic nature of business and how quickly things can change. Companies who refuse to learn are frequently caught off guard when change or a shift in market needs does occur. These companies suffer from paradigm paralysis, what some describe as "hardening of the attitudes." Paradigm paralysis can be caused by insecurity, by willful complacency, or sometimes by cognitive dissonance.[13]

> Don't let your schooling get in the way of your education.
>
> MARK TWAIN

The simple truth of Superperformance can only be received by "ears that hear." Organizations that cannot understand or hear the simple truth of Superperformance are forced to cling to an outdated paradigm—Machine View. This is a self-limiting worldview, a shrinking currency of diminishing returns.

Continuing to operate in willful ignorance is a recipe for disaster. Knowledge, like market conditions, customer preferences, technology, and competitive advantage, evolves. "Best practice" is a moving target. Organizations that refuse to learn will eventually die out.

Organism View recognizes that organizations are living, complex adaptive organisms. Ceaseless learning is an infinitely wiser, surer path to long-term success and optimization.

SUPER REMEDY

Become a learning organization to increase adaptability.

Undertaking Transformation

Everyone must participate in the transformation of the system. Everyone involved needs a sober appreciation for the psychological and physical complexities of change. Acquiring new habits requires discipline. There is no shortcut to transformation. Single events alone do not create sustainable new ways of being. What is required is a systemic approach. It must catalyze short-term results while simultaneously creating an enduring new way of being.

To change into something different is to acquire new habits. Habits govern 99.997% of our steady state.[14] By trading sub-performing habits for Superperforming habits, any organization can undergo the metamorphosis to Superperformance. The transformation plan should allow an organization to move at its own pace, to expand or contract activities as needed, while retaining the consistent, long-term focus that is essential.

The ideal plan for a phase transition to Superperformance should be based on the consistent partnership of process and culture, comprehensive management and leadership development, reconfiguration of corporate systems to support the new organization, systemic improvement projects driven by key stakeholder requirements, organic application, and the development of specialized internal consultants. (For a more detailed implementation blueprint, see Appendix 1.) The blueprint that follows provides a way to test changes on a small scale before embarking on organization-wide deployment. It can be universally tailored to company-specific goals, strategies and operating structures.

Upshifting to Superperformance

When a caterpillar is ready to become a butterfly, it forms a chrysalis and its metamorphosis begins. In the same way, when an organization is ready to become a Superperformer, it must take certain steps to get the transformation underway. Here are nine simple steps to bring about a phase transition to Superperformance. These steps can be applied at

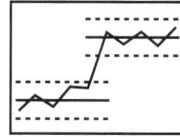

EMERGENCE

New Steady State
New way of life
Super results
Continuous Oscillation

At the Tipping Point (Order ←→ Chaos)
- *Small inputs can become huge outputs*
- *Signifcance precedes awareness*
- *The environment is catalytic*
- *Complexity is greatest in:*

Phase Transition

Metamorphosis
Trade old paradigm and habits for new paradigm and habits.

  ◆ *Interactions*
  ◆ *Novelty*
  ◆ *Diversity*
  ◆ *Energy*

Apply the Rules, Implement the Superperformance Formula
PxC=SP

Super Vision

Current State

The Emergence of Superperformance

any scale in an organization: department scale, division scale, or entire company scale. They are universally adaptable. And they are repeatable. The steps are designed to move an organization further along the Superperformance learning curve over time.

They will work today, and they will work many years from now. The purposefulness with which each step is undertaken will determine the ultimate outcome of that particular learning cycle.

1. Provoke the transformation of key individuals.

2. Create a call to action.

3. Develop a Super vision.

4. Assess the organization's current state.

5. Develop an internal Superperformance Consultant (SPC) agency.

6. Implement enterprise projects to transform flow and unleash passion.

7. Implement continual learning.

8. Evaluate and act to hold the gains.

9. Align formal structures and processes.

1. Provoke the Transformation of Key Individuals

A system-level transition to Superperformance cannot occur without new knowledge. Transformation of an organization requires first the transformation of key individuals, and this comes from understanding what Superperformance is, how it happens, and accepting that it is a real possibility for the organization. This is a critical first step. Unless key individuals are fundamentally changed, a system-level transformation is virtually impossible.

This change is a sort of phase transition on a personal level; the transformed key individual, operating out of a new paradigm, will adopt new habits and apply new principles. As Deming pointed out, this will change the way he or she interacts with others, with systems, and with new circumstances. These interactions form the catalyst for organizational Superperformance. Key individuals typically include chief executives, board members, chief operating officers, and other senior executives.

Once transformed, these people will live in a different world, attaching new meaning to process and culture, leadership and management. They will model new behaviors, act differently, teach others, and emphasize new things. They will move to accelerate transformation drivers and remove transformation barriers. Their actions will influence others to transform. Then, as more and more individuals are transformed, these interactions will increase, driving the organization to the tipping point of Superperformance.

> The first step is transformation of the individual. This transformation is discontinuous.... The individual, transformed, will perceive new meaning to his life, to events, to numbers, to interactions between people.
>
> W. EDWARDS DEMING

2. Create a Call to Action

A call to action is more than a call to do something different; it is a call to *be* something different. People need to recognize that Superperformance is a real possibility for the organization. They need to know that achieving Superperformance will mean the organization and everyone in it can become much more than anyone previously dreamed possible. A call to action is an *infusion* of energy; it is the spread of enthusiasm for a new possibility.

This process is legitmized through conversations, with individuals looking carefully at where they are today and recognizing that Superperformance is a legitimate future state.

The questions that follow help to determine how ready an organization is for Superperformance. Everyone involved, from executives, to operating managers, to employees, to board members, should consider these questions about the organization from the perspective of his or her unique role— and the involvement that role requires.

1. Does the organization understand Superperformance?

2. Does the organization know its purpose? Does this purpose

arise from shared values? Does it guide the work of the organization?

3. Is the organization a great place to work?

4. Does the purpose address evolving customer needs? Or do gaps exist between the organization's purpose and the requirements of its customers?

5. Does the organization actively support the application of best practices for transforming process and liberating culture?

6. Is the organization committed to the systematic and continuous collection of data about its customers, processes, and culture, and does it use the data to improve?

7. Is everyone equipped to effectively use relationship skills, facilitation skills, teambuilding skills, and engagement skills in interactions with others?

8. Is everyone equipped to effectively use process improvement skills, project management skills, lean manufacturing skills, and systems and statistical thinking skills in interactions with process?

9. Do formal leadership and management have the support and involvement of the workforce?

10. Does the workforce have the support and involvement of formal leadership and management?

11. Do people at every level have appropriate and ongoing opportunities for management and leadership development?

12. Is the organization's main financial and operational plan based on a long-term vision?

13. Does the organization's reward system promote everybody-win? Are gain sharing practices linked to the organization's overall success in achieving its purpose and priorities?

    14. Does the organization have an effective governance system, which fortifies the long-term interaction of process and culture?

Use ongoing conversation to engage everyone, to help the workforce to acquire a deep appreciation for the power of the Superperformance principles. Assure buy-in from everyone by fully explaining the relationship of Superperformance to the organization's unique business case.

3. Develop a Super Vision

Creating a vision of Superperformance requires everyone's involvement. The key question to answer is, "How would this organization look if it were everything it could be?" The Super vision is the answer to that question. The vision should include how the organization will look in the context of the company's industry, associates, customers, shareholders, community, processes, products, and customers. A Super vision will excite everyone.

4. Assess the Organization's Current State

There are multiple ways to assess the current steady state of organizational process and culture. Some important measures are profitability, customer satisfaction, turnaround time, costs, process complexity, employee fulfillment, personal and company values alignment, interdepartmental cooperation, and level of engagement.

5. Develop an Internal Superperformance Consultant (SPC) Agency

Sometimes a full-scale improvement methodology is required. When project issues are of major strategic importance, when they affect multiple company functions, or when they contain complex analytic requirements, it's time to call in the experts. Every organization must develop its own experts for these larger challenges—its own agency of Superperformance Consultants (SPCs).

In leading and managing projects, these SPCs make sure to leverage both process and culture. (See Appendix 2.) Experienced external consultants can be brought in as needed to help with certification, coaching, and guidance of SPCs. External consultants can provide SPC development, facilitate initial project reviews, and provide coaching services to maintain forward moving progress. But it is imperative that an agency of SPCs be fundamentally homegrown.

You must unlearn what you have learned.

The approach to developing Superperformance Consultants in tandem with project work is called an *Action-Learning* model.

MASTER YODA, JEDI KNIGHT

The model combines capability development with real-time project implementation. SPCs are mentored as they learn.

Ideally, these agents are developed in multiple segments over several months, similar to the training process for traditional Quality Black Belts. At initiation, SPC candidates are assigned specific performance transformation projects and teams (based on the outcomes of Superperformance planning processes). As candidates complete each segment of learning, they immediately apply the concepts and tools they acquire to relevant organizational projects, mentored as they go by an assigned external consultant.

6. Implement Enterprise Projects to Transform Flow and Unleash Passion

The key to Superperformance is taking the long view. This means selecting and prioritizing projects that will yield the highest systemic impact over time, while acquiring new habits and discarding old ones.

It is important to match the appropriate methodology to specific improvement projects. Not every project warrants the rigor of a full-scale project methodology. Superperformers often utilize other less complex methods to improve performance levels, such as rapid cycle process improvement. Simple methods and small-scale testing can be used to pick the low hanging fruit (the easily identified improvement opportunities) in an organization throughout the first several cycles of application.

Once beyond these simpler projects, the statistical process management techniques and other tools learned by SPCs become more appropriate for improving performance levels.

A great time to positively impact the culture of an organization is during project work. This is an opportunity to directly engage people, raise their inspiration, passion, and involvement. This focus on a real project adds the essential energy of cultural engagement to the transformation experience.

SPC projects are an opportunity to transform flow and unleash passion. As they work through their projects, project teams should receive just-in-time and just-in-context training in relevant management and leadership skills. This balance of equal parts special projects and organic application and equal emphasis process and culture is a new approach for most organizations.

> It's not so much that we're afraid of change or so in love with the old ways, but it's that place in between that we fear. . . . It's like being between trapezes. It's Linus when his blanket is in the dryer. There's nothing to hold on to.
>
> MARILYN FERGUSON

7. Implement Continual Learning

Not only must senior executives model new habits and behaviors, they must promote continual learning. Top executives must set the tone for the new organization and for the new way of being. What are some important areas to consider?

Authenticity—People know the difference between a real desire for something different and the flavor-of-the-month version of change. People want to know that there is real caring for them as individuals and an authentic, long-term commitment to change. Senior executives should truly care for those they lead, and care about the organization they are changing.

Involvement—As Stephen Covey emphasizes, "No involvement, no commitment."[15] Everyone should have a real voice in the change. Superperformance cannot thrive in a paternalistic organization. Senior executives should involve those they are leading in bringing about change.

Symbolism—What you do is more important than what you say. Simple symbolic gestures that reflect the new "way of being," a new vision, can speak volumes. Senior executives should examine themselves to assure they actually are walking the way they are talking.

Engagement—Leaders must get buy-in, so that everyone in the company feels a personal sense of responsibility for bringing about the organization's success. Senior executives should help everyone feel that they have a stake in the outcome.

Humility—A servant's heart is a powerful force that can change the most immovable object. Senior executives should be servant leaders.

Discernment—Programmatic approaches are a poor substitute for thoughtful intervention. The objective should be to look for teachable moments, intervening just-in-time and just-in-context. Senior executives should discern when the moment is right to instruct and intervene.

Practicality—The transformation to Superperformance requires practicality. Transformation is a long-term undertaking operating in tension with today's reality. Senior executives should find practical solutions to adjust to changing conditions.

Systemic Improvement—The most important focus of improvement should be the overall system. Although some projects may not extend beyond individual components (divisions, departments, etc.), the consistent aim should be to improve the system. Senior executives should work holistically on the system.

Customer Focus—The voice of the customer should drive the process. Understanding the relationship of customer needs to specific parts of the process is critical. Senior executives should know their customers' needs.

Strategic Transformation Projects—Major projects should be undertaken for their long-term strategic value. Senior executives should take on projects that will most influence the company's long-term transformation goals, and assure that those projects are managed well.

8. Evaluate and Act to Hold the Gains

Once a change has been successfully implemented, act to "hold the gain," to prevent the inevitable slide backwards. Then syndicate successful changes throughout the organization. Use ongoing and detailed evaluations.

Evaluation measures should be consistent throughout organizations. Just as vital signs are universal measures of a person's health, an organization needs global measures of its health. An organization can use a Vector of Measures, or set of metrics (consisting of approximately seven to ten system indicators). A Vector of Measures creates a common language, making it easy to communicate performance so that everyone can understand the company's strategic plan and system performance evaluation process. These measures cascade down into an organization, relating to work in every area. Everyone should be able to understand how the work of his/her department or group relates to one or more of the global measures.

> In God we trust. All others bring data.
>
> W. Edwards Deming

To monitor the ongoing health of the system, it is important to check its vital signs regularly. By using a system-level Vector of Measures, it is possible to see changing patterns over time. This is a fundamental tool.

Since the organization's optimum health is affected by both process (tangibles) and culture (intangibles), a Super-balanced scorecard must include both tangible and intangible measures. Many companies already use a system performance scorecard incorporating operational, financial, and stakeholder satisfaction measures. Some additional metrics to consider include company rate of learning, interdepartmental cooperation, employee fulfillment and engagement, innovation rate, and alignment of personal/company values.

In general, organizations with a Vector of Measures, "Dashboard," or "Scorecard" already in place would benefit greatly from increasing the weight of intangibles.

9. Align Structures and Planning Processes

An important concluding requirement is the alignment of company structures and adoption of an ongoing planning process to sustain the new steady state. Components of this step may include, but are not limited to:

- Alignment of human resources policies and practices.
- Installation of ongoing planning processes.
- A system-level performance function.
- Ongoing assessment and reporting of process and culture results.
- Ongoing customer needs assessment, project selection, and prioritization.
- Procedural and technological mechanisms for tracking projects and project results.
- Communication strategies within the organization.
- Appropriate reward, recognition, and incentive programs.
- Ongoing career development for Superperformance Consultants.

Summary

- To upshift to Superperformance is to undergo a phase transition. This transformation requires a second-order change, which fundamentally changes a system, creating something new and unprecedented.

- Superperformers avoid performance appraisal and forced ranking, short-term thinking, wrong CEOs, weak ethics, mergers, and learning disabilities.

- Transformation to Superperformance begins with transformation of key individuals. Once transformed, the key individual will see a different world, attach new meaning to process and culture, leadership and management.

- Individual transformation leads to new habits and behaviors, which change the nature of interactions between individuals and others, and between individuals and the environment.

- Organizations that want to upshift to Superperformance should consider organizational readiness, investigating both transformation drivers and barriers.

- To monitor the ongoing health of the system, it is important to take its vital signs regularly. By using a global Vector of Measures, an organization creates a common language and focus, making it easy to communicate performance so that everyone can understand how his/her work relates to the larger system. To evaluate both process and culture, a Vector of Measures must include both tangible and intangible measures.

- Organizations that want to upshift to Superperformance can follow the nine step plan presented in this chapter.

8 Simple Rules

Chapter 8

Sustaining Superperformance

Living in Balance (Holding the Tension)

The surest way to maintain a steady state of Superperformance is to remain in balance. This is easier said than done. Because they are *polar-complements*, process and culture live in a natural tension, ceaselessly shifting back and forth between two opposing poles. This makes Superperformance an eternal balancing act.

In this state of persistent disequilibrium, things are constantly being shaken up as the system acts to conform to a constantly *de*-forming environment. At the same time an underlying order must prevail, providing sufficient structure so the system can maintain its identity and purpose. It is precisely through this paradox (of conflicting goals) that maximum adaptability is achieved.

The trick is to hold the tension.

An organization that has drifted too far left (*over-control*) will suffer from bureaucratic, inflexible structures; diminished individuality; and stagnant creativity. The remedy is to go right—improve culture—to bring the system back into balance. This could take the form of renewing

IF OVERCONTROL ⟶ *go right*

Rigidity & Bureaucracy
Diminished Innovation
Diminished Individuality
Devalued Intangibles
Overemphasis on process

Renew Engagement and Involvement
Renew Leadership Development
Revise Human Resource Practices
Engage Creativity and Diversity

go left ⟵ **IF UNDERCONTROL**

Refocus
Renew Management Development
Simplify and Improve Process
Institute Project Management
Institute Understanding of Patterns

Chaos and Confusion
Entitlement
Lack of Organization and Focus
Overemphasis on Culture
Devalued Tangibles

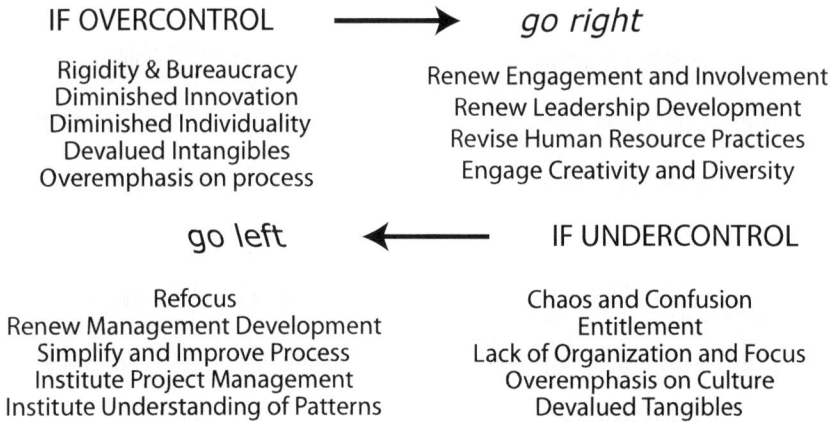

the engagement and involvement of people; revising human development practices; or nourishing intrinsic motivation, creativity, and fun.

On the other hand, an organization that has drifted too far right (*under-control*) will reflect chaotic processes, ad-hoc structures, and a pervasive sense of entitlement. In this case what is called for is a left turn—improve process to bring the system back into balance. This might include refocusing, documenting the organization's critical linkage of processes, standardizing improvement methods, or using statistical principles to guide decisions.

RULE 8: Superperformers Oscillate to Continue Superperforming

By oscillating between process and culture, Superperformers are able to maintain optimum fitness indefinitely. A Superperforming system is an oscillating system.

Why is this so? Oscillation is the inherent pulse of nature. Imagine oceans without waves or life without a heartbeat. By instinct all living systems work to attain equilibrium, but by design never actually attain it.

Hence the biological classification of living systems as "non-equilibrium" systems. (A system that has attained a state of complete equilibrium will also be a dead one.) Biologist Bertlanffy (from Chapter 2) coined a special German term, *Fliessgleichgewicht* (for "flowing balance") to describe this steady state of non-equilibrium in open systems.[1]

Because polar-complements are interdependent, it sub-optimizes the system to choose one and ignore the other. Breathing is often cited by Eastern philosophers as a great illustration of this principle. Inhaling and exhaling are both helpful; however, if you only focus on either inhaling or exhaling alone, breathing is not sustainable. This does not

> # What is the sound of one hand clapping?
> Zen Riddle

mean that either inhaling or exhaling is inherently bad. It simply means that both together form one interdependent whole, each requiring the other for completion.[2]

A Final Note: Redefining Corporate Learning

For an organization to become everything it can be, corporate learning must become everything it can be.

The traditional cause-and-effect model of corporate learning is governed by a mechanistic paradigm. Its false assumptions are based on the idea that schooling is learning. But schooling isn't accountable to learners; it isn't practice-based or connected to real life. Schooling is all advocacy, no inquiry. Its guiding principles are based on these misguided notions:

- Learning is passive and incremental.
- Learning is acquired information.
- Potential and capability are limited.
- Everybody learns in the same way; one size fits all.
- Content coverage and replication are the aim.
- Learning is defined by the calendar and the amount of time.
- Learning is non-participative.

Schooling is sub-optimal learning. Schooling approaches human development with the same mentality that pushes widgets through production lines. People and organizations are containers to be filled with the necessary information, on a strict schedule. But as William Butler Yeats said over a century ago, "Education is not filling a bucket, but lighting a fire."

Informed corporate learning recognizes that learning is emergent and that people and organizations are living, complex adaptive organisms, not machines. And organisms learn best by doing. Therefore, "super" learning must involve communities of interaction as well as direct practice. Super learning recognizes several truths:

- Learning is dynamic; strategy adjusts to the current situation.
- Learners construct their own meanings.
- Learning requires interaction.
- Learning potential is unlimited.
- Learning is enhanced with creativity and play.
- Learners determine their own path.
- Effectiveness can be qualitative, not just quantitative.
- Situational learning is better than passive learning.
- Live practice is essential.

What to Learn

Superperformance requires new capabilities for both leading people and managing process. Blended learning strategies, which integrate live practice, action-learning models (real world experience), and direct application, work best. The following curriculum should be implemented.

Transforming Flow— Management of Process

- *Focusing*—Delineation and Use of Core Purpose, Aim of the System

- *Improving*—Continual Improvement, Use of Tools, Design and Tests of Change

- *Simplifying*—Lean Principles, JIT, and Removing of Waste

- *Project Management*—Structuring, Chartering, and Monitoring Projects

- *Statistical and Systems Thinking*—Flow, Linkage of Process, Patterns, and Control Charts

UNLEASHING PASSION—LEADERSHIP OF PEOPLE

- *Encouraging Others*—Understanding Emergence, Inspiration, Liberating Intrinsic Motivation

- *Enrolling Others*—Involvement of the Individual, Aligning Values and Purpose

- *Relating to Others*—Understanding Nonlinear Interactions, Cooperation, Relationship Skills, Group Facilitation and Emergence

- *Innovating*—Understanding Self-Organization, Creativity, Change

- *Living in Integrity*—Understanding Self-Reference, Integrity Levels

The Ramifications of Superperformance

The simplicity of Superperformance is almost too fantastic to believe. Yet it is true. From Toyota Motors to Southwest Airlines, Superperformance is the fruit of extraordinary process interacting with extraordinary culture. How is it that so many organizations have missed such an obvious opportunity? At least part of the answer is that they cling to an obsolete management science to guide behavior.

> We struggle with the complexities and avoid the simplicities
>
> NORMAN VINCENT PEALE

The new science of Superperformance is a life science. It introduces

139

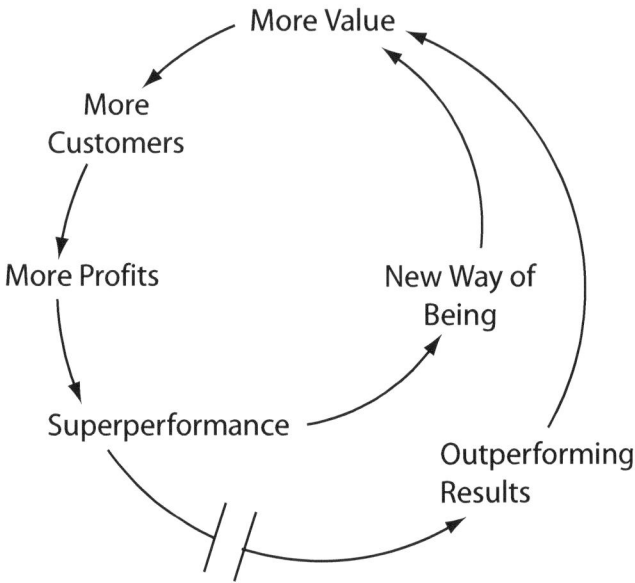

The Superperformance Value Proposition.

a simple new understanding of organizations as organisms—living, complex adaptive systems—with the same polar-complementary nature that works in other organisms. It reveals a new organization, a new reality, and a provocative, highly explanatory new performance paradigm to guide behavior.

The ramifcations are significant. Superperformance is nothing short of new profound knowledge for corporate leaders. By adopting and applying these few simple principles, it is possible to achieve and sustain unprecedented performance levels. One simple formula, eight simple rules, one billion great results. My prayer is that you and your organization find great utility in this knowledge.

Summary

- Because they are *polar-complements*, process and culture live in persistent tension, continuously shifting back and forth between two opposing poles. By remaining in balance, an organization can sustain a steady state of Superperformance indefinitely.

- An organization that has drifted too far left (overcontrol) must go right—improve culture to bring the system back into balance. Conversely, an organization that has drifted too far right (undercontrol) must go left—improve process to bring the system back into balance.

- Superperformers reinvent corporate learning to move from a learning-by-schooling model to a learning-by-doing model. They make use of new blended strategies, which integrate live practice, action-learning models, and direct application.

- The ramifications of Superperformance are significant. By adopting and applying these few simple principles, it is possible to achieve and sustain unprecedented performance levels.

8 Simple Rules

RULE 1: Process x Culture = Superperformance

RULE 2: Superperformers superperform over time

RULE 3: The paradigm shift of Superperformance is from
Machine to Organism

RULE 4: Superperformance is produced by super management and
super leadership

RULE 5: Superperformance is transformed flow

RULE 6: Superperformance is unleashed passion

RULE 7: Superperformance requires metamorphosis

RULE 8: Superperformers oscillate to continue superperforming

Appendix 1

The Superperformance Transformation Blueprint

A number of requests made to Corpus Optima for a more detailed transformation and learning plan led to the development of this Superperformance Transformation Blueprint, a systematic approach to acquiring Superperformance through the creation of new processes, habits and interactions. This model plan is designed to help organizations more fully ignite and operationalize the journey to Superperformance, and can be implemented by any organization. It is being used today by large and small companies to drive and sustain unprecedented new levels of quality and performance excellence.

As a core element, the plan includes a process for developing internal Superperformance Consultants (see Appendix 2) to deploy and perpetuate these principles throughout organizations. Through structured learning, project work, coaching/mentoring, and on-the-job application, these transformation agencies can be prepared to pursue and sustain the application of Superperformance methodologies throughout any enterprise.

Systemic Approach to Superperformance

This system transformation model is a multi-phased process

characterized by repetitive PDSA learning cycles, major projects driven by key stakeholder requirements, organic application, and internal capability building. It is of course necessary to tailor the blueprint to company-specific goals, strategies and operating structures.

The three major phases are Discovery, Deployment, and Evaluation:

DISCOVERY	DEPLOYMENT	EVALUATION
Organizational Assessment	Certifying Internal Consultants	Evaluation and Continuous Learning
Leadership Education	Deploying Projects	Aligning Structures
Transformation Planning	Global Education	Planning for Sustainability
Establishing Key Metrics	Organic Application	

Discovery Actions

Form and educate an influential group of formal leaders, middle managers and front-line workers in the principles of Superperformance and provoke a call to action. Create a shared vision and enrollment strategy for Superperformance that will engage and involve every employee. Assess organizational performance and create key metrics and transformation objectives for process and culture. Align business strategy and core business processes to key stakeholder requirements. Then create relevant, line of sight performance improvement targets, stretch goals and appropriate measures.

Deployment Actions

Using transformation teams, organic application, and a focused project management approach, enable everyone to take action. Implement new people practices designed to liberate intrinsic motivation. Recast major process transformation targets into a manageable number (approximately 5 to 8) of customer-focused projects. Organize transformation team efforts with clear charters, success criteria, rigorous reviews, and most of all, the power to act. Implement an appropriate level (one that can be supported over time) of organic process and culture enhancement activities. Communicate with and involve everyone in the transformation.

Evaluation Actions

Evaluate and take action as indicated to hold the gains or design new tests of change. Syndicate positive changes across the organization. Adopt a pervasive continual process and culture enhancement strategy and communicate it robustly to everyone. Drive projects to timely results. Achieve acceleration by employing an Action Learning methodology combining structured education with real-time project work to quickly bridge from learning to doing. Align structures to reinforce the transformation.

Overarching Elements

Implementation should include the following core elements:
- A deep appreciation for the power of the Superperformance principles and a call to achieve a new future vision of the organization as a Superperformer.
- A systematic approach that has actionable items to improve culture and process now, while at the same time supporting the necessary longer-term transformation process.
- Enough flexibility to adapt to a constantly de-forming environment.
- Skills development for formal leaders and managers to address new process and cultural challenges.
- A real understanding for the relationship between

Superperformance and the organization's unique business case, assuring buy-in from everyone.

- Change Leadership: A way for the organization to transition from the previous level of performance to a new way of being, one that demonstrates new levels of commitment to people and process.
- Support for the organization's Superperformance Consultants (SPCs) and teams to develop specialized capabilities for orchestrating large-scale projects.
- Education for all employees to develop new management and leadership skills that enable them to create the ideal culture and achieve new levels of process performance.
- Institution of a dynamic, practice-based learning system capable of systemically developing cultural and process enhancing habits throughout the organization, involving formal leadership, management, employees and Superperformance Consultants (SPCs).

The Transformation Campaign

The following chart and associated narration illustrates the specific strategies used in a transformation campaign. Note that throughout the entire campaign, there is a requirement for ongoing evaluation and feedback, allowing continuous adjustments to be made to support the transformation process.

1. The Organizational Assessment

The purpose of this segment of work is to establish the baseline state of an organization's process and culture. Typically, the three main components of this segment include (1) review of existing system performance information, (2) individual and group interviews with key stakeholders, and (3) use of various tangible and intangible performance assessment tools (such as Corpus Optima's Readiness for Superperformance Questionnaire, and Superperformance Quotient Derivation Instrument

Superperformance Transformation Blueprint

Ongoing Organization Analysis

(Balanced Scorecard)

Culture

- Employee Engagement
- Turnover
- Communications
- Cooperation
- Work-Life Balance
- Learning Development
- Career Development
- Fulfillment

Process

- Flow
- Customer Satisfaction
- Cost Reduction
- Cost Avoidance
- Inventory Turns
- Timeliness
- Simplicity

Performance

- ROI
- Profitability
- Market Share
- Share Price
- Cash Flow
- Etc.

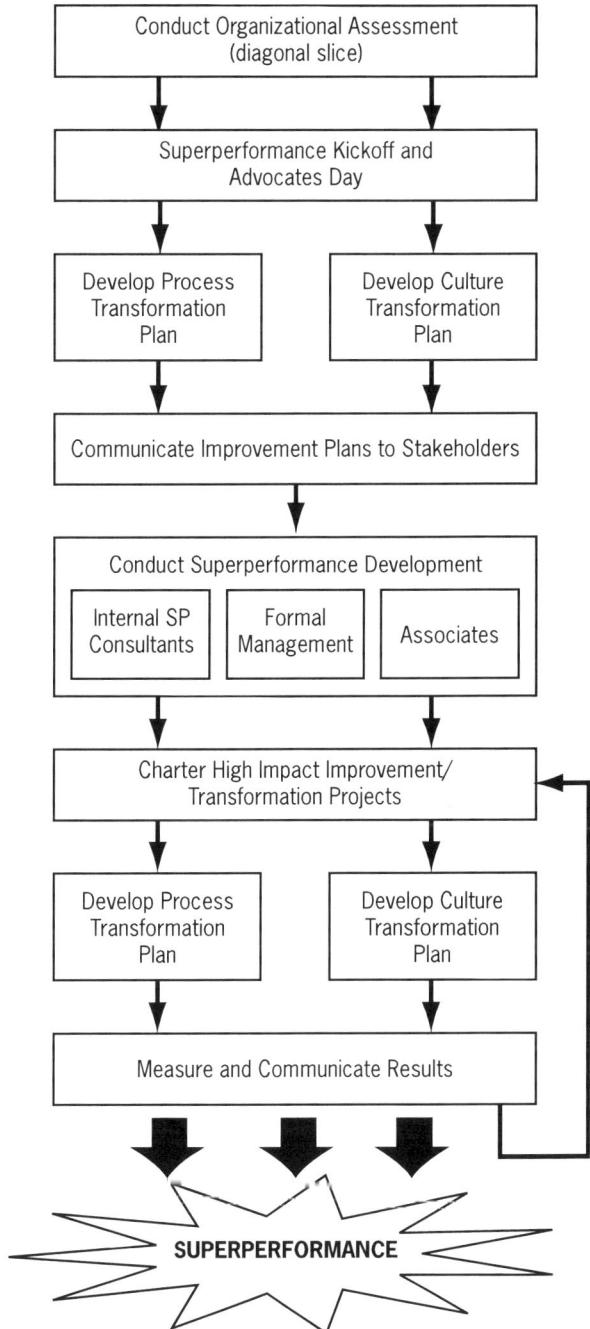

Conduct Organizational Assessment (diagonal slice)

Superperformance Kickoff and Advocates Day

Develop Process Transformation Plan

Develop Culture Transformation Plan

Communicate Improvement Plans to Stakeholders

Conduct Superperformance Development

| Internal SP Consultants | Formal Management | Associates |

Charter High Impact Improvement/ Transformation Projects

Develop Process Transformation Plan

Develop Culture Transformation Plan

Measure and Communicate Results

SUPERPERFORMANCE

147

[SQDI]). Armed with this knowledge, an organization will know what strengths it can leverage to accelerate transformation, as well what areas of special difficulty will need to be addressed throughout the campaign.

During the assessment, evaluation measures are developed to enable the organization to have continual feedback throughout the transformation campaign.

2. The Superperformance Kickoff Retreat

A Superperformance business transformation campaign must be aligned with business strategies and supported throughout the organization. The Superperformance Kickoff retreat creates this alignment and establishes the support that will energize the campaign. Typically, influential leaders gather for a multi-day session to:

- Understand how Superperformance happens.
- Discuss the business case for Superperformance.
- Create shared understanding of the organization's strategic business goals and ways that a shift to Superperformance can support these goals.
- Create a call to action.
- Discuss the key criteria for success associated with Superperformance.
- Install a balanced scorecard or vector of measures.
- Identify key Superperformance projects for implementation in the organization, and determine the appropriate methodology for each.
- Allocate resources for identified projects.
- Plan for communicating change associated with Superperformance.

3. The Advocates Day

Radiating a new way of being throughout an organization means providing each level in the organization with the new skills and knowledge required for successful implementation. Once alignment and buy-in are initiated in the Superperformance Kickoff Retreat, the next phase involves preparing Advocates to support the Superperformance projects that will be executed within their areas. Superperformance Advocates should control required resources, own the affected process portfolios, and commit to conducting ongoing project reviews with the SPC and the Superperformance project teams.

During this day of development, Advocates receive an overview of the learning that will ultimately be delivered to Superperformance Consultants. Advocate development focuses on the tools and methods that will be used, and their application within continual process improvement and cultural transformation projects. In particular, Advocates learn how to lead differently within the context of a Superperformance environment, and to effectively support project teams. The Superperformance Advocates Day is designed to help Advocates meet the following objectives:

- Understand the organization as an organism.
- Understand performance and the various tools applied for continual improvement.
- Create appreciation for the critical role of an inspired culture to bring about desired change.
- Determine appropriate application for various improvement tools and methods.
- Define criteria for selection of Superperformance Consultants.
- Manage the change campaign associated with Superperformance projects.
- Plan support required for Superperformance projects in the organization.

Although project selection and prioritization begin in the Superperformance Kickoff Retreat, final project selection, project chartering, and resource allocation is ideally completed during the Advocates Day. The projects are evaluated based on customer requirements, analysis and issue complexity, and are matched to the appropriate methodology.

149

4. Superperforming Management and Leadership Education

Superperforming Management and Leadership Education is a way to cascade Superperformance approaches and techniques throughout an organization. This process emphasizes: (1) Understanding Superperformance, (2) Understanding the Habits of Superperforming Management and Leadership, (3) A structured methodology for undertaking organic process improvement and cultural transformation, and (4) Use of intermediate Superperformance tools within that methodology.

This level of skills and knowledge enables everyone to dramatically increase personal effectiveness, support the transformation, become cultural leaders and process managers, function as high performing members on Superperformance project teams, as well as valued participants on projects that do not require the Superperformance level of analysis and rigor.

All employees complete a multi-day blended learning process. This experience is designed to provide participants with an overview of Superperformance as well as practice new methods associated with effective application, including transferring this knowledge to daily work. A large part of the practice focuses on the use of rapid cycle performance improvement and cultural best practices. This highly interactive and hands-on experience is designed to accomplish the following objectives:

- Bring into organic use a proven method for accelerating improvement.
- Broadly apply a highly effective, scalable, and robust improvement model.
- Increase personal awareness, emotional intelligence, and relationship skills.
- Acquire a new portfolio of skills for leveraging teams, workgroups and communities of practice.
- Develop the high level of involvement required for success in a Superperforming environment.

- Create high energy and involvement for positive change.

The fundamental premise of this approach is that transformation begins with the individual, and that the solution to most issues resides with process owners, those individuals who work with an issue on a daily basis. These people are the real heroes of the revolution, and will make change happen if they are freed from the boundaries that typically stifle participation and intrinsic motivation; and if formal management is willing to lead by listening and respond quickly to employee generated improvement proposals. To move to a new steady state everyone must go to work on the transformation.

This application is fundamentally an action accelerator. It bridges the gap between high-level systemic improvement work and implementation of organization-wide action to achieve transformation. This level of blended learning and practical application is the right approach anytime and anywhere:

- there is an authentic organizational desire for Superperformance.
- there is a culture in place that encourages and celebrates bottom-up involvement.
- there is a clear and well-defined system purpose.
- there is application of a robust performance improvement method or tool.
- there are employees who can provide know-how, creativity and energy to accelerate ideas for achieving improvement.

Superperforming Management and Leadership Education does not replace other improvement practices such as rapid cycle process improvement, statistical thinking, teambuilding, relationship skills and process documentation. It is designed to take the output of these tools and leverage that knowledge to create and execute practical action plans that convert knowledge into action. All positive results or recommendations can be syndicated across the organization with an approach to implementation at the lowest level possible by the individuals closest to the action.

5. Foundations of Superperformance

Foundations of Superperformance is a way to orient new employees, suppliers, and other stakeholders to the principles and basic concepts of Superperformance. Foundations of Superperformance is designed to assure continued alignment and support throughout the organization and its stakeholders over time. This segment can be tailored to introduce new employees, board members, shareholders, suppliers and other interested stakeholders to Superperformance and the basic theory and practice that underlies it. This typically single day learning experience can also serve as a prerequisite to Superperforming Leadership and Management Education. This hands-on, interactive session accomplishes the following objectives:

- Understand what Superperformance is and how to get it.
- Discuss the key criteria for success associated with Superperformance.
- Create shared understanding of the organization's strategic business goals and how a shift to Superperformance can support these goals.
- Understand Distributed Leadership and Management.
- Overview of the 10 Habits of Superperformance.

6. Deployment of Both Key Projects and Organic Application

The path to Superperformance involves both High-Level Projects and Organic Application. High-Level Projects are deployed through an Action Learning approach and supported by Superperformance Consultants (SPCs). Action Learning combines experiential practice with real-time project implementation and mentoring. External consultants and internal SPCs provide the structure and guidance during high-level project work that enables every project interaction to be both educational and fruitful. In between meetings, project team members receive further guidance as needed to continue the cultural and process transformation.

High-level project work also furthers the development of the organization's Superperformance Consultant Agency (See Appendix 2). The company's cadre of Superperformance Consultants should be viewed as a key vehicle in the transformation to Superperformance and have a continuing role to play in sustaining the new steady state.

Organic application involves everyone in acquiring the habits of Superperformance and applying the principles of Superperformance to daily work. This involves use of methodologies such as rapid cycle process improvement, and concepts of lean operations and small scale testing. In addition, organizations must enroll everyone continually in their shared responsibility for leadership in creating a new culture that unleashes passion and helps everyone to become everything they can be.

Short-Term Results

Although short-term results of any Superperformance transformation are not the most critical outcome, they do matter. The timeframe for achieving short-term results depends on organizational complexity and appetite. Almost any company can show an initial bottom-line result, but the most important, real issue is the sustainability of these gains and the creation of the new culture. This abbreviated Superperformance Transformation Blueprint is geared to accelerate business transformation through the implementation of an enterprise-wide process, certification of Superperformance Consultants, deployment of high-level projects and organic application, development and involvement at every operating level, and use of external resources as needed.

The Superperformance Consultant

Superperformance Consultant Description

The transformation of flow and the liberation of culture can be accelerated through the use of an internal agency of Superperformance Consultants (SPCs). SPCs are a new breed of improvement agency, equipped to surf the corpus callosum of the organization's left and right brain. They uniquely serve as both a performance execution agency and a cultural ministry. These are the new, more highly-adapted foot soldiers of Superperformance. These performance masters are different from traditional Quality Black Belts in several ways:

Servant-Mindedness

The process owners are the customers of SPC services. Process owners know more about the process under scrutiny than anyone else. The SPC is in place to guide and assist their improvement efforts, not to assume ownership of their process. Credit for any improvements that are made should go to the process owner and the team, not to the SPC. (This is the antithesis of prevailing practice.) The ancient Chinese proverb, "The master craftsman leaves no trace," is an appropriate guiding principle.

Knowledge Sharing

SPCs are knowledge sharers, not knowledge hoarders. Knowledge has power, but it has infinitely greater power (and greater value to the organization) if it is shared. SPCs remain on the leading edge of learning by participating in a community of practice with other SPCs in their company and with SPCs in other companies. This larger community is a living, sharing organism that enlarges its own knowledge capital by promulgating best practices among its members. The SPC should also share his or her knowledge with process owners as they engage in project work, although it is not expected that the process owners will reach the knowledge level of the SPC with respect to the improvement tools.

Cultural Ministry

The Superperformance Consultant is not only a technical specialist, but also a model of civility, integrity, and emotional intelligence. SPCs model positive interpersonal interactions, which are evident in their success in engaging and enrolling others, and their expert use of relationship skills, team skills, and creativity skills. The SPC teaches this new way of being to others. SPCs understand the science behind Superperformance, including elements of complexity (CAS) and biology.

The Superperformance Consultant Charter

The charter of the SPC is to foster the transformation of flow and the liberation of culture within her/his organization. In the transformation, the SPC must keep in mind the good of the organization as a whole, and avoid the pitfalls of improving one area at the expense of another. The SPC will also recognize that his/her role is one of continuously learning and sharing.

Capabilities of the Superperformance Consultant

The SPC operates from a robust process improvement model to transform process and culture. As such, the SPC must be capable of performing the actions necessitated by the model. The following are the capabilities of the SPC with examples of how those capabilities are used.

Provide Presentations and Consultation in Statistics/Understanding Variation

FORMAL PRESENTATIONS:

SPCs deliver multi-day workshops for groups or teams tailored to the specific applications/processes of the client. These workshops, applicable to manufacturing, engineering, and service process, include the following topics:
- The basics of the theory of variation.
- How variation causes loss in the processes of the organization and in processes of their customers.
- Feature set (of the company's products and services).
- Selection of important characteristics.
- Low cost methods of monitoring those characteristics.
- Using the data to guide improvements.

INFORMAL DEVELOPMENT

SPCs hold private consultations on the same subjects, with coaching, follow-up, data analysis, and interpretation support.

Plan, Design, and Interpret Analytic Statistical Studies (e.g., formal experimentation, statistical process management methods)

BASIC INTERVENTION

Assist a team in planning a simple, basic experiment (generally four or fewer factors at no more than 2 levels, where a high level of current knowledge exists), conducting the experiment, and guiding the interpretation of the results. During the experiment, the SPC provides learning experiences that teach the concepts related to experimentation.

ADVANCED

Guide a team through a more complicated attempt at process improvement, generally involving more than four (possibly multi-level) factors that must be varied simultaneously. Using the event, the SPC helps the team understand the "trade-offs of potential interventions" and make decisions based on those trade-offs.

Support Process Management and Superperformance Methodology

SPCs will work directly with teams (special project teams or process teams) to:

- Provide an overview of the general principles of Superperformance.
- Facilitate the team through chartering (establishment of what they are trying to accomplish), assembly of current knowledge, and testing changes to determine if they are improvements.
- Enable the team to use improvement tools on a "just in time" basis, and to help them know when they need to use a particular tool or need expert help with one.
- Refocus/dislodge a "problem" team, or a team that has lost focus.

Mentor/Coach Team Leaders

SPCs spend additional time with team leaders in a mentor or coach role. During this time, they will.

- Show team leaders how to lead a team (responsibilities, methods, etc.).
- Model servant leadership.
- Mentor/coach team leaders as they work with their team/run their business.
- Teach team leaders how and when to use basic tools, and when to ask for help or advice.

- Share scientific principles behind Superformance as needed.

Manage the Performance Improvement Model and Cultural Enhancement Methods

Each organization will customize the performance improvement model and cultural enhancement methods for its own use. The SPC's efforts to manage the model and methods include:

- Maintain responsibility for the latest performance improvement model structure for the company.
- Continually improve the model by incorporating lessons learned into the performance improvement knowledge base.
- Assure the use of cultural best practices.
- Actively seek to educate employees on improvement of process and culture through course offerings, articles, and blended and action-learning approaches.

Promote a Product/Service Life Cycle Management Process

SPCs move among the product groups to promote product/service life cycle management activities. Specifically they:

- Educate employees in the general approach to creating a product or service development and life cycle framework/process. The presented approach will be flexible, will allow for differing product or service family complexity, and can be tailored to the needs of differing business entities within the company. The approach is updated frequently to reflect learning.
- Facilitate the tailoring of the company process to the needs of specific business units. Include follow-up, and create examples and models specific to business units and/or education for appropriate personnel (i.e., marketing, design, manufacturing).

158

Teach the Use of Performance Improvement and Culture Enhancement Tools

SPCs understand well that tools are best learned when they are needed. With that understanding, they:

- Work directly with teams to guide them in the use of specific process and culture improvement tools, and help them understand when and how to use the right tool at the right time in the context of the improvement model and presenting circumstances.
- Provide templates and reference materials as appropriate for teams and individuals to enable them to know when a tool is needed and to use it effectively.

Obtain Information Through Surveys

Surveys provide SPCs with valuable information on the current state of process and culture, and in how well employees are using tools and exhibiting habits related to Superperformance. The SPC can:

- Determine whether or not a survey is appropriate, and explore other options.
- Plan, conduct, interpret, and act on the results of the survey (use the survey in a PDSA cycle).

Implement Inspection Economics

The level of inspection and test of incoming material viewed is an economic decision. How do we achieve lowest total cost? Should we inspect 100%, 0%, or something in between? SPCs assist in answering these questions using proven statistical techniques to provide lowest total cost to the company. Inspection economies are applicable to manufacturing and non-manufacturing processes, and include key characteristic determination, understanding variation of those characteristics, and risk/ Failure Mode Effects Analysis (FMEA).

Developing Superperformance Consultants

Organizations should develop internal SPCs. The goal should be to arm SPCs with mastery not only of important improvement tools and methods for the transformation of flow (process), but also mastery of skills that provoke the inspiration and engagement of people (culture), by facilitating the emergence of teams, creating a shared future vision, and leading system change.

SPCs are developed over time. The SPC development model typically proceeds through the multiple phases of a real project. Each phase builds on the previous, providing instruction and specific mentored assignments to grow mastery in the twin dimensions of Superperformance, while at the same time transforming a strategically important area for the organization.

Appendix 3

Superperformance Assessment

This abbreviated Superperformance Assessment Tool can be used to estimate the current state of an organization's process and culture to target initial improvement efforts. A more complete assessment tool (such as Corpus Optima's Superperformance Quotient Derivation Instrument [SQDI]) should be tailored to organization-specific process and culture dimensions, as well as contain a weighted score based on the prevailing polar-complementarity of process and culture, to provide a more robust evaluation of an organization's prevailing state.

Low scores in either culture or process, or a large difference between the culture and process scores, show where the critical opportunities lie.

CULTURE	*(Circle a number)*
	Low . . . High
Employees are empowered with responsibility, authority, and accountability.	1 2 3 4 5
Employees feel a sense of ownership for the company.	1 2 3 4 5
Employees care about each other.	1 2 3 4 5
Employees are encouraged to grow to new heights.	1 2 3 4 5
Leaders help rather than try to control people.	1 2 3 4 5
Ideas and differences are welcomed.	1 2 3 4 5
People are recognized for their contributions.	1 2 3 4 5
This is a great place to work.	1 2 3 4 5
Organizational gains are shared equitably with employees at all levels.	1 2 3 4 5
Employees are treated with fairness, dignity, and respect.	1 2 3 4 5
Work-life balance is encouraged and actively supported.	1 2 3 4 5
Results are achieved through teamwork and cooperation.	1 2 3 4 5
Employees are assigned to positions based on aligning motivations with job requirements.	1 2 3 4 5
Employees are kept well informed of the organization's goals, plans and results.	1 2 3 4 5

TOTAL (Add up the circled numbers)

PROCESS	(Circle a number) Low . . . High
The organization has a clear, shared purpose.	1 2 3 4 5
Employees understand the company as a system.	1 2 3 4 5
Employees understand how their work fits into the work of the company.	1 2 3 4 5
Employees have identified their key processes.	1 2 3 4 5
Employees are involved in improving their key processes.	1 2 3 4 5
Removal of waste is an ongoing persuit in all areas of the company.	1 2 3 4 5
There is a defined improvement method at work throughout the company.	1 2 3 4 5
Statistical thinking is used to guide decision-making.	1 2 3 4 5
Customer feedback is a core driver of improvement projects.	1 2 3 4 5
Project management skills are used to drive key projects.	1 2 3 4 5
Gain sharing emphasizes system performance.	1 2 3 4 5
Employees undergo development of process improvement capabilities.	1 2 3 4 5
There are opportunities to advance learning.	1 2 3 4 5
The company has in place a balanced set of metrics for monitoring system performance.	1 2 3 4 5

TOTAL (Add up the circled numbers)

Notes

Preface

1. Rothschild, Michael, *Bionomics: Economy as Ecosystem* (New York: Henry Holt, 1990).

2. Wheatley, Margaret, *Leadership and the New Science* (San Francisco: Berrett-Koehler Publishers, 1992).

Chapter 1: How Superperformance Happens

1. Ornstein, Robert, *The Right Mind: Making Sense of the Hemispheres* (New York: Harvest Books, 1998) pp. 43-60.

2. Kitterle, Frederick L., *Hemispheric Communication: Methods and Models* (New Jersey: Lea Publishing, 1995).

3. Palmer, Martin, *Book of Yin and Yang: Understanding the Chinese Philosophy of Opposites* (London: Piatkus Books, 1997).

4. Pais, Abraham, *The Genius of Science* (New York: Oxford University Press, 2000) pp. 23-24.

5. Gleick, James, *Genius: The Life and Science of Richard Feynman* (New York: Random House, 1992) p. 40.

6. Bladel, Niels, *Harmony and Unity: the Life of Niels Bohr* (New York: John Konin, 1988).

164

7. Watson, James, *The Double Helix* (reprinted New York: Touchstone, 2001) p. 167.
8. Ibid., p. 182.
9. *Jung, Carl Gustav*, Microsoft® Encarta® Online Encyclopedia, 2004.
10. Lewin, Roger, *Complexity: Life at the Edge of Chaos. 2nd Edition.* (University of Chicago Press, 1999) pp 44-62. See also Langton, Chris, ed., *Life at the Edge of Chaos—Proceedings of the 2nd Conference on Artificial Life* (Santa Fe Institute, 1991); Packard, Norman, "Adaptation toward the Edge of Chaos," in: Kelso, J. A. S.; Mandell, A. J. & Shlesinger, M. F. (eds.), *Dynamic Patterns in Complex Systems* (World Scientific, 1998) pp. 293-301; Crutchfield, James P, Santa Fe Institute, "What lies between Order and Chaos?" in J. Casti, ed., *Art and Complexity* (Oxford University Press, 2002).
11. Clippinger, John Henry III, *The Biology of Business* (San Francisco: Jossey-Bass, 1999) pp. 8-9.

Chapter 2: The Business End of Superperformance

1. Lowenstein, Roger, *Buffett: The Making of an American Capitalist* (New York: Random House, 1995) pp. 46-48.
2. Currier, Chet, "Lean Market May Make Buffett Change Strategy," *Washington Post*, May 8, 2005 (Warren Buffett comments at Berkshire Hathaway Annual Meeting, April 30, 2005).
3. Buffett, Warren, "Berkshire Hathaway Chairman's Letter," 1989.
4. Ibid.
5. O' Loughlin, James, *The Real Warren Buffett: Leading People, Managing Capital* (London: Nicholas Brealey Publishing, 2003).
6. Miles, Robert P., *The Buffett CEO* (New York: Wiley & Sons, 2002) p. 260.
7. Kilpatrick, Andy, *Of Permanent Value, The Story of Warren Buffett* (Birmingham, Alabama: Andy Kilpatrick Publishing Empire, 1998) p. 1061.
8. Tilson, Whitney, "Corporate Culture Affects Profits," *Motley Fool*, August 21, 2001, http://www.motleyfool.com.

9. Filipczak, Bob, "The Soul of the HOG," *Training Magazine* (February 1996) pp. 40-42.

10. Reid, Peter C., *Well Made in America: Lessons from Harley Davidson on Being the Best* (New York: McGraw Hill, 1991) p. 70.

11. Luderer, Michèle, "Interview: Richard Teerlink made Harley's Engine Purr," Credit Suisse Forum, http://www.credit-suisse.com (March 3, 2003).

12. Pringle, Anna, "Microsoft Ireland – What Makes the Company a Great Place to Work?" *Discovery Research* (February 2004).

13. Pringle (2004).

14. Thielen, David and Shirley Thielen, *The 12 Simple Secrets of Microsoft Management* (New York: McGraw Hill School Education Group, 1999).

15. Pringle (2004).

16. Huey, John and Geoffrey Colvin, "Staying Smart," *Fortune Magazine* (January 11, 1999).

17. Freiberg, Kevin and Jackie Freiberg, *Nuts! Southwest Airlines' Crazy Recipe for Business and Personal Success* (New York: Broadway Books, 1996, 1997) p. 327.

18. Personal Interview, August 23, 2003.

19. Barrett, Richard, *Liberating the Corporate Soul* (New York: Butterworth-Heinemann, 1998).

20. "Letter to Shareholders," *SYSCO 2003 Annual Report* (SYSCO) pp. 12-14.

21. Liker, Jeffrey, *The Toyota Way* (New York: McGraw Hill, 2004) Forward.

22. Walton, Sam, *Sam Walton: Made in America* (New York: Bantam Books, 1993) p. 162.

23. Ibid., pp. 162-163.

Chapter 3: Machine to Organism

1. Kuhn, Thomas, *The Structure of Scientific Revolutions* (Chicago: University of Chicago Press, 1962) p. 149.

2. Gharajedaghi, Jamshid, *Systems Thinking: Managing Chaos and Complexity* (London: Butterworth-Heinemann, 1999) p. 10.
3. Taylor, Frederick Winslow, *Principles of Scientific Management* (New York: Harper & Brothers, 1911).
4. Personal Interview, September 5, 2003.
5. Rothschild, Michael, *Bionomics: Economy as Ecosystem* (New York: Henry Holt, 1990) p. 95.
6. Charles François, *History and Philosophy of the Social Sciences* (Argentina: GESI: Grupo de Estudio de Sistemas, 1992).
7. Capra, Fritjof, *The Web of Life* (New York: Anchor Doubleday, 1996) p. 48.
8. Ludwig von Bertalanffy, *General System Theory: Foundations, Development, Applications* (New York: George Braziller, 1969) p. 92.
9. Ibid., p. 93.
10. Ibid., p. 55.
11. Prigogene, Illya, and Isabelle Stengers, *Order out of Chaos* (Boston: Shambhala Press, 1984) p. 143. See also Prigogene, Illya, and Isabelle Stengers, *The End of Certainty: Time, Chaos and the New Laws of Nature* (New York: Free Press, 1997) pp. 66, 70.

Chapter 4: Leading and Managing Superperformance

1. Yasuda, Yuzo, *40 Years, 20 Million Ideas: The Toyota Suggestion System* (New York: Productivity Press, 1990).
2. Gallup Corporation, *Q12 Survey*, 2003.
3. Drucker, Peter, *Managing in the Next Society* (New York: Truman Talley Books, 2002) pp. 126-127.
4. Drucker, Peter, *Management Challenges for the 21st Century* (New York: Harper Books, 2000) p. 22.
5. Langley, Gerald, Cliff Norman, Lloyd Provost, Tom Nolan, and Kevin Nolan, *The Improvement Guide* (San Francisco: Jossey-Bass, 1996) p. 6.
6. Clippinger, John, *The Biology of Business* (San Francisco: Jossey-Bass, 1999) Forward by Esther Dyson.

7. James, William, *Talks to Teachers on Psychology* (Cambridge: Harvard University, 1899) Chapter 8.

8. Kauffman, Stuart, *At Home in the Universe* (Oxford: Oxford University Press, 1995) pp. 149-189.

Chapter 5: Transforming Flow

1. Aguayo, Rafael, *Dr. Deming, The American who Taught the Japanese about Quality* (New York: Carol Publishing Company, 1990).

2. Deming, W. Edwards, *The New Economics* (Cambridge: MIT Press, 1993).

3. Deming, W. Edwards, *Out of the Crisis* (Cambridge: MIT Press, 1989) p. 19.

4. Deming, W. Edwards, *The New Economics* (Cambridge: MIT Press, 1993) p. 110.

5. Ibid., p. 124.

6. Ibid., p. 58-60.

7. Ackoff, Russell, *Ackoff's Best: His Classic Writings on Management* (Hoboken, New Jersey: Wiley, 1999) pp. 15-18.

8. Deming, W. Edwards, *The New Econonmics* (Cambridge: MIT Press, 1993) pp. 58-60.

9. Deming, W. Edwards, *Out of the Crisis* (Cambridge: MIT Press, 1989) p. 86.

10. Langley, Gerald, Cliff Norman, Lloyd Provost, Tom Nolan, and Kevin Nolan, *The Improvement Guide* (San Francisco: Jossey-Bass, 1996) pp. 3-11, 50-59.

11. Womack, James P., *The Machine That Changed the World: The Story of Lean Production* (New York: Simon & Schuster, 1990).

12. Project Management Institute, *A Guide to the Project Management Body of Knowledge: PMBOK Guide* (Newtown Square: Pennsylvania, PMI, 2000).

13. Deming, W. Edwards, *The New Economics* (Cambridge: MIT Press, 1993) p. 60.

Chapter 6: Unleashing Passion

1. Luderer, Michèle, "Interview: Richard Teerlink made Harley's Engine Purr," Credit Suisse Forum, http://www.credit-suisse.com (March 3, 2003).

2. Hagstrom, Robert, *The Warren Buffett Way* (Hoboken, New Jersey: John Wiley & Sons, 2004) p. 80.

3. Arthur, Brian, "Positive Feedbacks in the Economy," *Scientific American* (February 1990). See also Arthur, Brian, "Increasing Returns and the New World of Business," *Harvard Business Review* (July-August 1996).

4. Frost, Peter and Sandra Robinson, "The Toxic Handler: Organizational Hero – and Casualty," *Harvard Business Review* (July-August 1999). See also Frost, Peter, *Toxic Emotions at Work* (Boston, Harvard Business School Press, 2003).

5. Peters, Tom and Robert Waterman, *In Search of Excellence* (New York: Harper Collins, 1982). See also Peters, Tom and Nancy Austin, *Passion for Excellence*, (New York: Random House 1985); Collins, Jim and Jerry Porras, *Built to Last* (New York: Harper Collins, 1994); Collins, Jim, *Good to Great* (New York: Harper Business, 2001); Kotter, John and James Heskett, *Corporate Culture and Performance*, (New York: Free Press 1992).

6. Hillenbrand, Laura, *Seabiscuit, An American Legend* (New York: Random House, 2001).

7. Goleman, Daniel, "What Makes a Leader?," *Harvard Business Review* (November-December 1998).

8. Goleman, Daniel, *Emotional Intelligence*, (New York: Bantam Books, 1995).

9. Liker, Jeffrey, *The Toyota Way* (New York: McGraw Hill, 2004) pp. 36, 298.

10. Kilpatrick, Andy, *Of Permanent Value: The Story of Warren Buffett* (Birmingham, Alabama: Andy Kilpatrick Publishing Empire, 1998) p. 395.

11. Moffitt, Nancy, "Defining Crisis Management," *Wharton Alumni Magazine* (Summer 2002).

Chapter 7: Upshifting to Superperformance

1. Lewin, Roger, *Complexity: Life at the Edge of Chaos, 2nd Edition* (University of Chicago Press, 1999) pp. 51, 54-55.

2. Deming, W. E., *Deming Library, Volume 19, Profound Knowledge for Leadership*, CCM Productions, New York. See also Deming, W. E., *Foundation for Management of Quality in the Western World. An Introduction to Total Quality for Schools* (Arlington, VA: American Association of School Administrators, 1990).

3. Russell, Sharman, *An Obsession with Butterflies* (Boulder, CO: Perseus Publishing, 2000).

4. Brower, Lincoln, *Inside the Chrysalis* (Journey North: Annenberg, CPB Science in Focus Series, 2001).

5. Coens, Tom, and Mary Jenkins, *Abolish Performance Apprasial: Why They Backfire and What to do Instead* (San Francisco: Berrett-Koehler, 2000) p. 18.

6. Personal Interview, September 5, 2003.

7. Barnet, Richard, and Ronald Muller, *Global Reach* (New York: Touchstone, 1976).

8. "For Motorola's Zander, 'It's Execution!'" *Business Week* (August 2, 2004). See also Goodman, Robin, "Organizational DNA: Cracking the Code on Execution," *Business Week* (May 27, 2004); Charam, Ram, "Why CEOs Fail," *Fortune Magazine* (June 21, 1999).

9. Lucier, Chuck, Rob Schuyt, and Junichi Handa, *CEO Succession 2003: The Perils of Good Governance* (Booz Allen Hamilton strategy +business, Summer 2004).

10. O' Loughlin, James, *The Real Warren Buffett: Leading People, Managing Capital* (London, Nicholas Brealey Publishing, 2003) pp. 19-28.

11. Serwer, Andy, "Dirty Rotten Numbers," *Fortune Magazine* (February 4, 2002).

12. Marks, Mitchell Lee, *Making One plus One equal Three in Mergers, Acquisitions and Alliances* (San Francisco: Jossey-Bass, 1997) pp. 3, 47.

13. Festinger, Leon, *A Theory of Cognitive Dissonance* (Stanford, CA: Stanford University Press, 1957).
14. James, William, *Talks to Teachers on Psychology* (Cambridge: Harvard University, 1899) Chapter 8.
15. Covey, Stephen, *The 7 Habits of Highly Effective People* (New York: Fireside, 1989) p. 143.

Chapter 8: Sustaining Superperformance

1. Capra, Fritjof, *The Web of Life* (New York: Anchor Doubleday 1996) p. 48.
2. Nyanapokina, N. Thera, *The Heart of Buddist Meditation* (New York: Weiser Books, 1973).

Index

Z

The Superperforming CEO

LIBERATING *the* PROMISE WITHIN

———

Uncommon Sense for Uncommon Results

———

DAVE GUERRA

About the Author

Dave Guerra is the originator and leading exponent on the theory and practice of Superperformance and the founder of the Superperformance movement. Dave regularly addresses and consults with executives from some of the world's leading companies, and conducts Superperformance seminars for a wide variety of corporate audiences.

He is also the founder and CEO of Corpus Optima, a consulting, coaching and education company specializing in Superperformance. Corpus Optima leverages the best of improvement and complexity science to help organizations leverage process and culture together. As the firm that pioneered the practice of Superperformance, Corpus Optima is the leading authority for the implementation of Superperformance-based business transformation initiatives. The firm's clients include many of the world's leading companies.

Over several decades, Dave has consulted extensively in the areas of servant leadership, continuous improvement, lean, and the use of complexity principles to transform corporate culture. He speaks passionately and frequently about the association between amplified process and culture and long-term industry outperformance. As the principal investigator and promulgator of Superperformance, he has discovered that its principles can be successfully applied to both organizations and individuals. He has authored numerous white papers and is currently at work on several additional books on the subject.

Dave and his wife Jodi and five children live in Houston, Texas.

To learn more about Superperformance and the Superperforming CEO, visit the Corpus Optima website at www.corpusoptima.com.